Dedication

This book is dedicated to my Young Living team. The honor of reaching the highest rank in Young Living goes to you. Without you, I am ordinary. Together, we are extraordinary!

Thank you for your dedication to service, to changing the way the world thinks about healthcare and for helping so many families improve their financial health.

I love you with all of my heart.

Your wave is GIGANTIC!

Contents

Acknowledgements

I want to express my appreciation for several people, beginning with D. Gary Young, the father of modern day distillation. Gary has been a mentor in every area of health and essential oils. He has often been a father figure to me and he has been a good friend. I cherish the times we have had together when Young Living was still small—on one occasion, Gary took me out to his garden and showed me his prize beets. Watching Gary grow into the world changer he is today inspires me daily! Thank you, Gary!

Next, I want to thank beautiful Mary Young. Mary came to Young Living with enormous business sense as well as high standards of style and beauty. From our hand-written labels and a handful of brochures to world-class labeling and exquisite colors, Mary has raised the Young Living brand to match the high quality of the products themselves. Mary is an inspiration to all of us.

My thanks also go to John Maxwell. His seventy best-selling books on leadership have educated and inspired people worldwide for decades. While I am blessed to have had many good mentors in my life, the things I have learned from John continue to have the most pivotal effect on my career and my life.

I am deeply grateful for John's heart, his faith and his ability to connect with cultures and nations. From the bottom of my heart, thank you John Maxwell.

Many of my business colleagues are aware that Beverly Banks has been my full-time Executive Assistant for many years. Not only has Beverly been a loyal and trustworthy employee, she is rapidly becoming a successful entrepreneur in her own right.

During the very little free time that Beverly has, she is always learning! Beverly is a self-motivated person who is always coming up with innovative ideas. She is never afraid to try a new ideas and she is not afraid to fail. This is the perfect recipe for success.

I would like to say a very special thank you to Beverly for offering innovative ideas to make this book even better. Unfortunately, there will come a day when Beverly will no longer be able to work for me, as she is choosing to build her own Young living business now. I predict she will go all the way to the top!

With love and gratitude for each of you.

Introduction

Welcome to an exhilarating journey of creating and expanding your influence in the areas of health, business and leadership with Young Living! The purpose of this book is to help brand-new and intermediate Young Living business owners create a solid plan for success.

As you tap into the inside details surrounding some of the innovative marketing ideas my team and I have implemented, it is my hope that you and your team create even more innovative ideas!

Take a moment and ponder this thought: Job security is never found in the job itself, rather in the person who is willing to continually grow and expand.

In my previous book, *How to Be a Stunning Success in Network Marketing*, I share the reasons I believe this is the best industry to be in for today's entrepreneurs. This book—*How Big is Your Wave?*—is specific to growing and building a highly successful business with the company Young Living Essential Oils.

I wrote this book in three sections, the first being How Big Is Your Health Wave? You may be wondering why I included a section on health in this book.

I believe that good health is a lifelong journey. Your health is the foundation of everything that occurs in your life—and your business performance is directly related to your level of health. As we work with Young Living products, our health knowledge will increase. When we consistently apply that knowledge to our own health, we stay strong for the journey and are able to help even more people along the way.

In the middle section, How Big is Your Business Wave?, I share the step-by-step activities that my team and I do with every new person we bring into our business followed by a complete marketing strategy for you to consider.

Just as a chair cannot stand on only two legs, a good marketing plan needs several well-thought-out activities all going at the same time to maximize success. This section is not meant to be a strict guide, rather, a beautiful marketing symphony in which you get to choose which instruments you like to play!

Marketing is something you just get better and better at the more you do it, analyze your results, and do again!

Section Three, How Big is Your Leadership Wave?, is about becoming a good leader. Once you read it, you will have the tools you need to lead your team. There are several bonuses in this section. As a certified John Maxwell Leadership trainer, I share some of the most important leadership concepts with you that I learned from John and the other instructors in his school. These concepts have impacted both my business and personal life in such a profound way that it is hard to describe.

My road to achieving the highest rank in Young Living, Royal Crown Diamond, has been filled with adventure! Do you like adventure? If so, you are in the right place! If you like traveling the world, meeting new people, living on the edge—Young Living is the company for you!

Not only does Young Living offer the highest quality wellness products in our industry and one of the most generous compensation plans available, you can look forward to receiving a four-year "business degree" for FREE as you learn endless new business skills from members of your own team while you are earning money along the way!

While the critics of our industry are so busy trying to find fault with it, network marketing continues to grow more successful entrepreneurs every single week around the world when compared to traditional business models.

How big is your wave? As big as you can believe for! Let's take this ride together on the journey of a lifetime!

To your success with love!

Teri Secrest

Section One
How Big is Your Health Wave?

How Big is Your Health Wave?

The statistics are staggering! Childhood diabetes and childhood obesity are at epidemic stages in our country! We must take action now to stop this downward spiral for the next generation. Each one of us can be part of the solution.

As Young Living wellness messengers, we can educate our clients about the importance of good nutrition along with our Young Living supplements. Many renowned medical doctors have agreed that most diseases can be avoided by one simple decision—the decision to eat a healthier diet.

Parents have a great opportunity for about eighteen years to model and teach their children about good health. Now that my last child has entered college, I can honestly say that nourishing my children well was an ongoing commitment. I would not trade it for anything.

While helping my youngest son get moved in for his sophomore year in college, he declared, "Mom, can we go shopping at the health food store? Last year the dorm food was awful! I just want to eat all organic this year!" I just had to laugh!

You can affect thousands of people's lives just by living and being "in health" yourself! The best part is this will really help you as a Young Living business owner because people will be drawn to your vitality. Creating a health wave begins with our own health and the health of our families!

Three Ways to Stay Strong

1. Let's get walking!

Can you think back to the last time that you felt good, I mean really good, as in full of energy, positive attitude and ready for the day? I'd like to share a simple secret with you that many well-respected people throughout history have discovered that can literally elevate the way you feel physically and emotionally beginning today—walking!

Our beloved 16th President, Abraham Lincoln, declared that he made some of his most important presidential decisions while walking the hills of Springfield.

God created us to be walkers! Brisk walking is good for every system of your body; it cleans out your lungs, it helps to keep your hormones happy and, best of all, as you take in oxygen while you walk, suddenly you begin to feel emotionally better without even knowing why! Amazingly, modern science has discovered that one of the greatest causes of depression is a lack of oxygen to the brain. So, by walking, you are being proactive in supporting your emotions on a daily basis.

As a personal health and wellness coach, one of the saddest things I see on a daily basis is the growing percentage of obesity in our youth. This is tragic! We can change this and it starts in our own homes, with the choices we make. Even if you were raised in a family where your parents made unhealthy lifestyle choices, you can start a new legacy today!

Tips to get walking!

- Invest in a good pair of walking shoes that give you support.
- Talk to your family or friends and see if someone would like to be your "walking buddy". (Don't let this stop you though, as your walking time can be your praying and creative thinking time)
- Start with a shorter commitment such as twenty minutes, three to four times per week. Work your way up to forty-five minutes a day, five to six times per week, as you get stronger.

- Become very aware of "how" you are walking. By pushing off with your feet as you step, you get more speed, a good rhythm and firm up your calves.
- Park far away from the store. Take the stairs instead of the elevator.
- As a result of daily walking, I feel better today than I did in my twenties and so can you! Let's enjoy longevity *with* vitality!

Fact: Experts suggest walking 6,000 steps a day to improve health and 10,000 steps a day to lose weight.

Fact: Walking increases the oxygen uptake into the brain and help ward off depression.

Lunch in our office—a huge, live salad
and Ningxia Red®. Join us!

2. Choose healthy foods

Food Lovers Unite!

Sometimes in the network marketing industry, we tend to get going at such a fast pace, we end up overlooking our own health! So here are a few concepts from my health book, *Eating Out of Heaven's Garden*, to help you enjoy maximum energy!

- Health isn't everything, but without it, life is not worth very much!
- Life and death are in the power of our forks!
- The simple truth is that live foods add life to the body. Sugar-laden, dead foods produce death in the body.
- Adding Young Living Essential Oils to your water and to many of your recipes can add zest to your life while increasing the nutritional profile.

We cannot trade our own health for success.
Teri Secrest

Houston, we have a problem!

In the United States,
25% of all vegetables consumed are potatoes;
the majority are eaten in the form of French fries!

Houston, we found a solution!

Nature offers a cornucopia of colorful vegetables,
each containing different nutrients that are vital
for good health. It is imperative that we expand
our diets to include an array of colorful foods.

Exciting News About the Color of Foods!

We were born to eat a colorful diet! The color of our vegetables and fruit is a clue to their health benefit.

Red foods strengthen and protect! They contain iron for healthy blood, minerals for bones and teeth, antioxidants to support the immune system and every other body system.

Orange and yellow foods are high in vitamin A to protect vision and eye health. Antioxidants in orange foods protect and regenerate tissues for beautiful skin. The fiber keeps you regular.

Green foods build strong bones, boost the immune system and cleanse the digestive system. Plus, deep green, leafy vegetables have more calcium than milk!

Blue & purple foods rejuvenate cells. They have powerful antioxidants, which may protect against inflammation and reduce the risk of stroke or heart disease.

White foods are your white knights, protecting you with immune-boosting nutrition! They can act as natural antibiotics. Garlic is the #1 white food.

Fruits are the cleansers in the body and vegetables are the builders. Vegetables are king! Let's all add some more vegetables in our diet.

Secret Messages Found in the Shapes of Foods!

Research has validated that the shape of certain foods is a clue to their healing ability in the body.

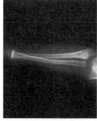 

The carotenoid in carrots promotes healthy eye function.

 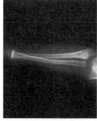

Celery is an excellent source of silica, which gives bones their strength.

 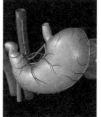

What to do for an upset stomach? Grab some fresh ginger and make yourself some tea.

Ripe, organic tomatoes help nourish the heart function; the lycopene in tomatoes reduces the risk of heart disease.

Fall in Love with the Humble Bean

Beans are loaded with vitamins, minerals and protein! They are easy on the budget, easy to cook and delicious! Beans are tops for weight loss—high in fiber and low in fat. Beans can reduce cholesterol, heart disease and many other health issues. Go ahead and try some new beans! Adzuki, lima, garbanzo, black, kidney, navy. . .the list is endless!

Fact: Kidney beans are shaped just like your kidneys and they are very good for kidney health!

Teri's Special Recipe for Burnout

Choose a large array of colorful, organic vegetables and place them in a soup pot with filtered water. Cover and bring to a boil.

Immediately, turn the heat down to low and simmer for two hours. Strain off the vegetables and drink the broth all day long. It will replenish your body with many important minerals.

Turn off your phones, cancel all of your appointments and just rest.

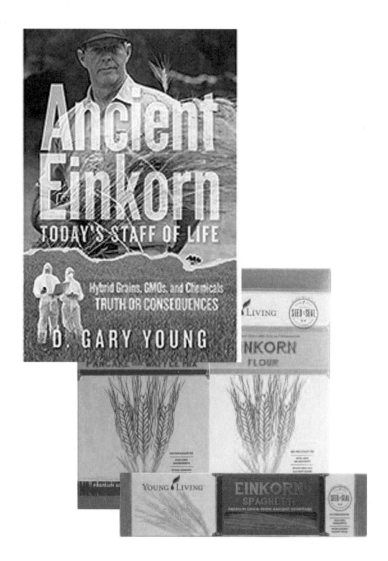

Fact: Gary Young is in the forefront of bringing back non-GMO, non-hybrid whole grains, starting with einkorn.

Ancient Grain is Today's Answer to GMO Grains
Introducing the most exciting ancient grain, rediscovered for today's modern health needs— EINKORN!

Einkorn wheat was one of the first plants to be domesticated and cultivated over 5000 years ago. Compared to modern wheat flour, whole grain einkorn is much more nutritious:

- Twice the vitamin A content
- 3-4 times more beta-carotene
- 4-5 times more riboflavin
- 3-4 times more lutein
- 20% lower glycemic index (65 vs. 85)

For the very first time, Young Living is making available three flagship products: Einkorn Pancake and Waffle Mix, Einkorn Flour and Einkorn Spaghetti.

Healthy Fats are a Must for Your Brains and Hormones!

One of the greatest mistakes the American people made in the last twenty years was going on a low fat diet! Not only did people become deficient in the important nutrients found in healthy fats, but obesity has increased instead of decreased!

Choose organic fats such as olive, avocado, safflower, sunflower, coconut, grapeseed and butter. Choose expeller or cold-pressed oils, as they have all the nutrition, aroma and flavor of the seed.

The best oils for cooking are coconut and grapeseed, because they do not break down when heated. Avoid unhealthy fats such as canola oil (GMO), margarine and hydrogenated oils.

Introducing Young Living's Natural and Delicious Sweetener—Agave Nectar

Most processed foods and drinks are heavily laced with high-fructose corn syrup. This sweetener is directly implicated in obesity, increased risk of diabetes, elevated blood pressure and many more health issues.

White sugar is also devastating to our health. It is highly acidic to the body, depleting minerals from bones and organs, can lead to high levels of blood fats and may raise the risk of heart disease.

> Fact: The most dangerous sweetener is
> high-fructose corn syrup.

We created a tradition called Fabulous Food Fridays, where all the guys in my youngest son's high school class were invited to a huge gourmet lunch! It was an epic adventure and THE place to be if you were anybody in that school!

Delicious, Home-Cooked Food is Minutes Away

Two big reasons why people don't eat healthy are they are intimidated by cooking at home and think it takes too long. Well, home-made meals can be as simple as you like and can be ready in less than thirty minutes.

I also think you'll discover how much fun you can have when you involve your family in the preparation. We've made so many happy memories in the kitchen and you can too!

Let's Get Chopping!

Learning to chop vegetables with a high-quality Asian-shaped knife is a powerful skill for your health! Remember, a dull knife is much more dangerous than a sharp knife, so keep your knives sharpened!

I'll bet I know what you are already thinking! "Teri, this is well and good, but we are a two-person working family and we do not have time to prepare all these healthy meals!"

He who knows how to chop vegetables quickly
will eat more vegetables. Teri Secrest

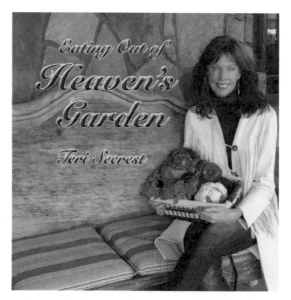

Five Simple Steps to Create a Healthier Lifestyle

If you are struggling with how to incorporate healthy meals for your family, here are five mindful steps you can take, starting today:

1. Get the junk out of your pantry or you'll eat it. Sugary cereals, drinks and junk food have to go!

2. Choose one day a week to plan the week's meals.

3. Choose another day when you can shop for that week's meals. Shop the perimeter aisles where the healthy foods are.

4. Increase the amount of raw foods you're eating by one cup a day.

5. Read Chapter Two of my health book, *Eating Out of Heaven's Garden*, and try one new recipe a week.

Introducing Young Living's Powerful Whole Food Supplements

When Young Living came out with Ningxia Red and a variety of delicious, essential oil-infused foods and supplements, I finally had a healthy solution to offer my friends and clients who didn't have time to cook.

Our Top Ten Supplements

Let's talk about the top Young Living products that are absolutely delicious and support the health of each body system.*

What sets Young Living supplements apart are the essential oils in them, which act as carriers, transporting the nutrients in the supplements, which makes them especially bio-available and easy for the body to assimilate.

I highly recommend that you put these products on your monthly Essential Rewards order to maximize your free product points. See page 83 to learn how you can receive free product.

What I've learned is that, by eating a healthy diet, our Young Living products work even better and faster!

*NOTE: The following statements have not been evaluated by the Food and Drug Administration. These products are not intended to diagnose, treat, cure, or prevent any disease.

Ningxia Red® Antioxidant Infusion

Ningxia Red is the foundational product of all the Young Living foods. It is the first nutritional building block upon which you will add your other Young Living supplements.

Ningxia Red juice will energize, fortify and revitalize the body and support overall health and wellness. It also supports eye health.

What sets Ningxia Red apart from all other antioxidant drinks on the market are the four citrus essential oils included in the formula. These essential oils are high in d-Limonene.

Master Formula

Master Formula is a foundational supplement that starts with essential food-based nutrients and then fortifies it with minerals, antioxidants, biotin and essential oils to support general well-being. Master Formula also includes prebiotics to support healthy gut flora and to help neutralize free radicals in the body.

This supplement is safe for those over the age of twelve who are looking for a full-spectrum, high quality multivitamin.

Pure Protein Complete
for Fast, Top Quality Protein

Pure Protein Complete

We love making shakes with Pure Protein Complete for breakfast and for healthy afternoon snacks. (Young Living has the best shaker bottle!) Pure Protein Complete is a comprehensive whey protein supplement that delivers 25 grams of protein per serving. It is high in protein and supports energy levels.

And now we have two new flavors—Chocolate Deluxe and Vanilla Spice. To make a shake, just add one or two scoops of your favorite flavor to your Young Living shaker bottle, add several ounces of organic whole milk or other beverage and shake. Try adding two ounces of Ningxia Red for extra flavor and nutrition.

MindWise for Brain & Heart

MindWise

Made from the exotic sacha inchi nut and a proprietary blend of nutrients, MindWise is a delicious, cold-pressed vegetarian oil.

MindWise has a high proportion of unsaturated fatty acids and an unmatched percentage of desirable omega-3 fatty acids. It also contains CoQ10, generous amounts of vitamin D3 and several other ingredients that support normal memory function as well as overall cognitive and cardiovascular health.

Sulfurzyme

Sulfurzyme

Sulfurzyme® combines wolfberry with MSM, a naturally-occurring organic form of dietary sulfur, which is needed by our bodies every day to maintain the structure of proteins, support healthy cell growth and cell membranes. It also supports the connections between cells and preserves the molecular framework of connective tissue. MSM supports a healthy immune system and liver, circulation and proper intestinal function, and works to scavenge free radicals. Wolfberries contain minerals and coenzymes that support the assimilation and metabolism of sulfur.

MultiGreens for Energy

MultiGreens

The thing I most appreciate about MultiGreens is its high-energy formula. MultiGreens is a nutritious chlorophyll formula designed to boost vitality by supporting healthy lymphatic, glandular, nervous and circulatory systems.

MultiGreens is made with spirulina, alfalfa sprouts, barley grass, bee pollen, eleuthero, Pacific kelp and therapeutic-grade essential oils.

Life 5 Probiotics for Healthy Digestion

Life 5

Healthy digestion is the key to overall vibrant health. Life 5 supports healthy digestion and intestinal health by providing five clinically-proven probiotic strains, including two advanced super strains to enhance intestinal health, sustain energy and improve immunity.

One Life 5 capsule contains ten billion active cultures and improves colonization up to ten times.

Minerals are Essential to Absorbing Vitamins

Mineral Essence

Two-time Nobel prize winner Linus Pauling Ph.D. states "You can trace every sickness, every disease and every ailment to a mineral deficiency."

Ionic minerals are the most quickly and completely absorbed form of minerals.

Mineral Essence is a balanced, full-spectrum, ionic mineral complex enhanced with essential oils.

Inner Defense for a Strong Immune System

Inner Defense

Formulated with the essential oils of Oregano, Thyme, Lemongrass and Thieves essential oil blend, Young Living's Inner Defense liquid softgels reinforce systemic defenses, promote healthy respiratory function and are rich in immune-supporting ingredients.

Longevity Supports Head to Toe Wellness

Longevity

Before Young Living created the brilliant formula for Longevity™, many of us spent tedious time filling our own capsules with essential oils.

Longevity softgels contain a powerful anti-oxidant blend enriched with essential oils of thyme, orange and frankincense. It also contains clove oil, nature's strongest antioxidant.

Longevity protects our DHA levels—a nutrient known to support brain function and cardiovascular health—promotes healthy cell regeneration and supports the liver and immune functions.

3. Get Some Rest

Adrenal gland exhaustion and insomnia are at epidemic proportions in America. As business owners, we must make a conscious choice to rest and relax every day. Good sleep is very important, as that's when our immune systems regenerate.

Creating a peaceful environment before sleep is important. Diffusing essential oils in your bedroom and turning off all electronics thirty minutes before bedtime should be your routine, as an overload of electronics can become an excitotoxin to your brain. Instead, try relaxing music for a beautiful sleep aid!

Fact: As health ambassadors, we need to model
good health habits to our customers
and business partners—including rest.

My Personal Health Commitment

Are you ready to make a renewed commitment to your personal health?

I, —————————————————— , make a commitment to make my health a priority and pass on the knowledge to others.

Beginning today, I purpose to add the following new health commitment to my current health regime.

—————————————————————————

Your signature

—————————————————————————

Date

Section Two
How Big is Your Business Wave?

How Big is Your Business Wave?

A few years ago, a successful businessman from Australia, by the name of Peter J. Daniels, came to America to speak—and he rocked my world!

He said what had made America great in her early years were two things: the unmerited favor of God and the entrepreneurs! He said the entrepreneurs started with a creative idea, rolled up their sleeves, went to work and did not quit until they were successful!

He reminded us that there were more innovative ideas brought forth during that time period than at any other time in history. He said that he had made 150 trips to America and that he was here with a warning! He said we have moved many of our businesses offshore and that too many people are depending on the government for a job or a handout! He said it is time for the entrepreneurs of America to stand up and take their place!

My Decision to Educate People About Our Industry

Up until this point in my Young Living career, I had never taught a single business class! While that says a lot about the high quality of our products and I am thankful to have thousands of happy product consumers, I now realize that our business is actually one of our very best products!

Friends, WE are the modern day entrepreneurs. WE are the solution to the current economic challenges! We have a brilliant business model that creates economic stability for our families and allows us the abundance to share with other people around the world.

Become Educated About Abundance

So what kind of business are we in with Young Living? We are in the wellness education business! We are also in the recommending business; we recommend products and services that we deeply believe in and love. Ultimately, what we are offering in Young Living is Wellness, Purpose and Abundance.

With all the negative talk in the media about wealth in the last few years, consider this reality: Capitalism feeds philanthropy!

Who fed the most people in the entire world in 2014? Bill Gates. Who is absolutely obsessed with eliminating world hunger? Richard Branson, owner of Virgin Airlines. I may not agree with their politics, but I sure agree with FREE enterprise!

Free enterprise feeds the world

Whoever came up with the idea that it is nobler to be poor was just plain misinformed! How are you going to feed the world if you are broke? How are you going to buy new car when your old one breaks down if you are poor?

Would you agree that money in the hands of good people is a very good thing? Free enterprise is the greatest system of economy the world has ever known and it is free enterprise that feeds philanthropy.

Developing Your Mindset of Abundance

The first thing a person must do in Network Marketing is overcome their own mindset of poverty or any mindset of lack that they have grown up with. I was very fortunate to come from a family of entrepreneurs. But if you did not come from a family like this, just remember that "Your history is NOT your destiny!"

As a women of faith, my experience over the last thirty-five years as a business owner is that God deeply cares about our financial health.

Allow me to share one of my favorite verses on this subject:

Beloved, I wish above all things that thou mayest prosper and be in health, even as thy soul prospers. III John 1:2

Let's examine all three parts of this verse: Not only does God care about our physical health, He cares about our financial health and the health of our soul. Many scholars define the soul to include the mind, will and emotions. The word, "even" is an important word here because it shows the importance of our soul prospering right alongside our health and our finances.

If we purpose to develop our soul, which includes our character, alongside of our physical and financial health, then we are more inclined to handle finances well. But if we gain financial wealth before our character develops, we see many examples in the world of people who do not handle abundance well.

Over the years, I've noticed that many good, hard-working Young Living distributors feel guilty about receiving money for their services. Some feel it's their calling to help others and that receiving money for it is wrong.

Does your doctor or dentist or drug store employee feel bad about cashing their paychecks? Of course not. They have done a service for people and they feel they have earned it.

So why would a Young Living business owner feel guilty about earning money for earnestly helping someone enjoy optimal health? It makes no sense, especially in light of the number of hours that dedicated wellness messengers put into their passion for helping people. To not receive the financial blessing associated with your efforts is, in my opinion, rejecting God's economy. This verse from I Timothy 5:18 drives the point home:

The laborer is worthy of his wages. I Tim 5:18

Money has never been the root of all evil, rather the love of money is the root of all evil. How sad that this verse has continually been taken out of context and has held so many good people in poverty for so many years. Spend time developing a healthy mindset about money because network marketing offers an opportunity for abundance like no other career in the world today.

The Law of the Lid

Our ability to accept and enjoy abundance is closely tied to the way we see ourselves. I learned the Law of the Lid from John Maxwell.

Ask yourself this question: How do you see yourself as a leader, on a scale of 1-10 with 10 being the highest?

My number is: _____

Here is how the Law of the Lid works: If you see yourself as a seven, for example, you have put an invisible lid on your success that will prevent you from exceeding that level.

Now, ask yourself how you can change your self-perception in order to go beyond the number you chose. Consider both leadership skills and self-image? Ask a trusted friend to help you bring that number up!

As a woman of faith, I sincerely believe that God sees you as a 10! What will it take to see yourself as a ten?

Organizational Structure
of a Traditional Corporation

It is corporate America that has a pyramid structure,
where only the very few can attain the top ranks.

Critics of Our Industry
Have it Backwards!

Compare the structure of corporations to the
brilliant business model of network marketing

Organizational Structure of a Network Marketing Business

Network Marketing has an <u>inverted</u> pyramid structure, where teamwork gains everyone the opportunity to reach the top ranks.

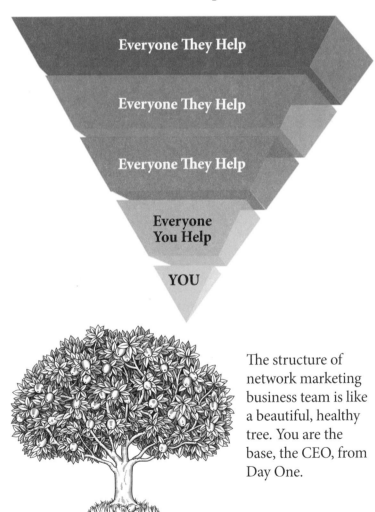

The structure of network marketing business team is like a beautiful, healthy tree. You are the base, the CEO, from Day One.

Identifying Your "Why?"

Discovering and identifying your "Why?" is the first thing you need to establish before you begin growing a Young Living business. Here are a few important questions you need to ask yourself:

1. Why are you interested in another stream of income? This question can come with a lot of emotion for people. Money is just a tool we use to get things accomplished.
2. What would you like to accomplish with it?
3. What are you are really passionate about that you currently cannot afford? Your "Why?" may start out being really practical, as in making an extra car payment or saving money for a vacation. Then, as your business grows, your "Why?" can expand.

4. It is whatever is on your heart today, what is motivating you. Remember, you can always expand it as you reach higher levels of success in Young Living and achieve some of your goals.

   Ultimately, your "Why?" may have little to do with money, but rather everything to do with a deeper longing in your heart.

   Remember though, as long as we live on the

earth, we still need to function in the world economy. So become very clear on why you would like to create a successful Young Living business. That "Why?" will keep you going when the going gets rough.

Write down your "Why?" below:

_____

_____

_____

_____

_____

Develop Dreams & Visions for Your Life

At Young Living, we get paid once a month. Imagine going to your mailbox, opening it up and seeing your Young Living check. You open the envelope and look at the dollar amount; that number gives you a feeling of accomplishment and deep satisfaction. You really feel like your Young Living business is successful.

What is that number for you? Hold that dollar amount in your mind and compare it to the following chart, which is the official Young Living Income Disclosure chart. At what rank on the chart does your number place you?

Look at your desired rank. In what time frame would you like to achieve it? How would it feel to look at your check and see that dollar amount?

What would a successful business add to your life? Also think outside of business. How would you really like your life to look?

How Big is Your Business Wave?

Member Rank	Avg Hours Worked Per Week	Avg Percent of Total Grouping	Avg Monthly Income	Avg Annualized Income
Star	5	62.2%	$73	$896
Senior Star	7	20.8%	$261	$3,132
Executive	11	12.1%	$617	$7,404
Silver	17	3.5%	$2,335	$28,020
Gold	23	1.0%	$6,527	$78,324
Platinum	32	0.3%	$15,721	$188,652
Diamond	45	0.1%	$32,003	$384,036
Crown Diamond	36	<0.1%	$57,300	$687,600
Royal Crown Diamond	37	<0.1%	$106,432	$1,277,184

The earnings of the members in this chart are not necessarily representative of the income, if any, that a Young Living member can or will earn through the Young Living Compensation Plan. A member's success will depend on individual diligence, work effort and market conditions. Young Living does not guarantee any income or rank success.

Create a Vision Board

A powerful way to work with your "Why?" and your dreams for your life is to create a Vision Board. Find a few photos and words that represent those things that you feel passionately about, those things that you desire in your life and your vision for your best self emerging and display them in a spot where you will see them every day. I recommend pinning the photos and words on your board with stickpins so you can remove an item as soon as you meet the goal or vision and replace it with new ones. Take several photos of your board and put them all over your home. It is imperative that you look at your dreams all day long.

My own vision board

Designing Your Day

Here are some realities to consider as you start your Young Living Business:

It takes seven to ten hours of dedicated time each week for two to five years to produce a six-figure annual income with Young Living. You may have to work more or fewer hours, but ten hours is the average.

How do you currently keep up with your time? Time management is an important business skill and an essential discipline to learn. If you already use a day planner, welcome to the minority! Keeping a schedule is a lost art in today's society. Most people make lists instead of intentionally planning their time.

What you really need is a day planner. Why? Because in network marketing, your day planner is your boss!

Until a few years ago, you could have called me a "shoot from the hip" person! Just the mention of a schedule made my heart rate go up. (Some of you may feel this way!)

When you take the plunge and begin to be intentional about your schedule, you will realize how much freedom it gives you. You will be able to

Your Day Planner is Your Boss!

Time	Activity	Time	Activity	Time	Activity
6:00	DRESS	2:00	CLIENT	10:00	SLEEP
6:15	BREAKFAST	2:15	WORK	10:15	8 hrs
6:30	READ &	2:30	1.5 hrs	10:30	
6:45	PRAY	2:45		10:45	
7:00	CLIENT	3:00	BREAK	11:00	
7:15	WORK	3:15		11:15	
7:30	3.5 hrs	3:30	FACEBOOK	11:30	
7:45		3:45	EMAILS	11:45	
8:00		4:00	PERSONAL	12:00	
8:15		4:15	& BUSINESS	12:15	
8:30		4:30	DEVELOPMENT	12:30	
8:45		4:45	& STUDY	12:45	
9:00		5:00	EXERCISE	1:00	
9:15		5:15		1:15	
9:30	BREAK	5:30		1:30	
9:45		5:45		1:45	
10:00	CLIENT	6:00	PERSONAL	2:00	
10:15	WORK	6:15	CALLS	2:15	
10:30		6:30	RELAX	2:30	
10:45	2 hrs	6:45	TIME	2:45	
11:00		7:00	MAKE DINNER	3:00	
11:15		7:15	&	3:15	
11:30		7:30	TIME WITH	3:30	
11:45		7:45	FAMILY	3:45	
noon	EAT	8:00		4:00	
12:15		8:15		4:15	
12:30		8:30	PERSONAL	4:30	
12:45		8:45	TIME	4:45	
1:00	WRITE BLOG	9:00		5:00	
1:15		9:15		5:15	
1:30	CLIENT WORK	9:30	BATHE	5:30	
1:45		9:45	GO TO BED	5:45	

focus on being present in each and every moment. As a matter of fact, you can unchain yourself from your email and cell phone while you are relaxing or spending time with your family, because now you choose to honor your free time!

How to Schedule Time for Everything

Here is your first assignment: Invest in a nice planner or select a scheduling app for your phone and take the following steps:

1. Schedule in your current obligations. For many people, that includes work. Some of you may be working a job and those hours have to go in first.

2. Next, write in all of your family activities. If your children are active in sports, if you or your spouse enjoys a hobby, write those down. Be sure

you include any weekly activities around your faith. Schedule friend time, fun time, reading time—even thinking time!

3. Last, but not least, write down your dedicated Young Living hours. The beauty of owning your own business is that you get to decide when to schedule those hours. You get to bend your working hours around your living hours.

However, this flexibility is not a license to be lazy or to make excuses! Some people are able to work two hours every day. Others are able to work five hours every Wednesday and Saturday. Whatever your designated Young Living hours are, schedule them and be as consistent as possible.

Once you have your hours scheduled, announce your business hours to your upline, your team and your family. Ask for their support. There is a lot of power in declaring that you are choosing to create a successful business and that you are committed to doing what it takes to be successful.

What to Do During Your Working Hours

A common mistake of new distributors is spending time on the wrong things. You can avoid that mistake by dividing your Young Living hours into an 80/20 split. Eighty percent of your dedicated

time should be spent interacting directly with current clients, gaining new clients and training business partners to do the same. These are the activities that put money in your pocket.

Twenty percent of your dedicated hours are spent doing the office tasks involved in running your business. This includes checking email, entering email addresses from your online duplicable marketing system, designing your business card and other important tasks involved with running your business. Consider these tips as you begin:

- You do not need your own logo to start a business.
- It is important to have a web presence; however it is not necessary to go to time and expense to design your own website. There are already several good systems out there to choose from.
- You do not need to create a unique name to start making money.

How to Create Abundance with Young Living

Now, for you to maximize your earning with Young Living, it is important for you to dive in and learn the terms we use everyday in our business. Let's go!

Terms That We Use Every Day

Enroller—The enroller is the person responsible for introducing the new enrollee to Young Living. They did the work of finding a new member and they are rewarded for that. The person listed as the enroller will receive the Premium Starter Kit bonus and the Fast Start bonus.

Sponsor—The sponsor is the person that you place your new enrollee under. You can choose to also be the sponsor of your new enrollee or you can strategically place them under one of your business partners to help begin building that leg.

Level—Anyone who you directly sponsor is considered to be on your first level. Any distributors sponsored by your first-level people are on your second level.

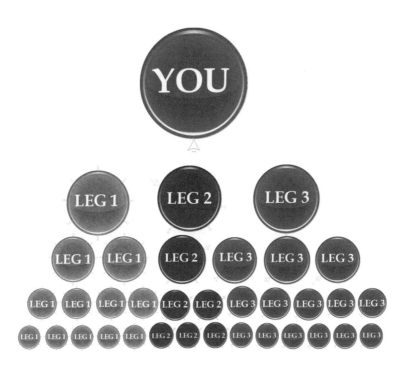

Leg—The number of people you personally sponsor will determine how many legs you have. When someone you sponsor begins to sponsor members, that becomes a leg.

Remember, in order to maximize the Young Living Compensation Plan, you only need six legs, although it is wise to build more.

Terminology about price and volume

There are three important numbers for every product:

1. The retail price
2. The wholesale price, which is the dollar amount you will pay for your products as a Young Living member
3. The personal volume or PV, which is the value Young Living assigns to each product—usually equal to the wholesale price. For some of the more rare essential oils, personal care products and marketing tools, the PV will not equal the wholesale price. All commissions are calculated based on Personal Volume.

Personal Volume (PV)

Personal volume is the sum total of the PV in your personal product order.

Organizational Group Volume (OGV) OGV is the sum total of all of the PV of your entire organization, including your PV.

Personal Group Volume (PGV)

Personal Group Volume doesn't become a factor until you reach the rank of Silver. However, it is still good to know in advance. PGV is the volume of your PV and the volume of those below you,

EXCLUDING any Silver or higher ranks and their volume.

It also EXCLUDES the volume from the legs that qualified you for the rank of Silver and above. Between the ranks of Silver all the way to Royal Crown Diamond, your PGV requirement will be $1000 each month.

The Fun Part: Getting Paid

It is also important to know how Young Living pays you. Young Living will pay you seven different ways. Below, let's discuss the first five ways, as they are important when you are first starting out.

1. Premium Starter Kit Bonus

You receive a $25 bonus for each new member you enroll who purchases one of the Premium Starter Kits. This bonus is a "thank you" for spreading the word about Young Living Essential Oils.

2. Fast Start Bonus

Young Living gives you 25% of the PV of each new enrollee for the first three calendar months of their membership. Then, every time your new enrollee signs up a new person, you receive 10% of that new person's PV for the first three calendar months after their enrollment.

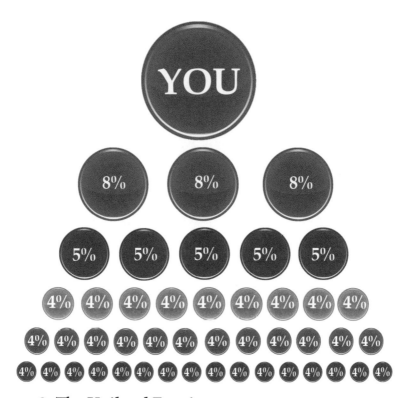

3. The Unilevel Earnings

This is where the "residual income" side of Young Living comes into play. Young Living pays you 8% of the PV on your first level, 5% of the PV on your second level, and 4% of the PV on your next three levels at the start of your business.

It only gets better from there! Take a look at this chart and see the income potential of the Young Living residual income. Note: You must qualify as an Executive or higher to be paid on all five levels.

4. Shares

Shares are at the beginning of what I call "free money." It's a bonus that Young Living will pay you and you don't have to do any extra work to earn it.

Young Living takes a percentage of 100% of the commissionable volume of the entire company worldwide and divides it up amongst distributors who have earned shares.

5. The Rising Star Team Bonus

This is how you earn shares while you are developing the foundation of your business. You earn the shares by simply structuring your company in a way that makes you more successful.

When you are maximizing the Rising Star Team Bonus, you will be earning a total of six shares and you will have the perfect structure to launch into the leadership ranks.

The commissions from shares are paid out monthly. The dollar amount of the shares varies from month to month but traditionally when you are earning the full Rising Star Team Bonus, you are making the equivalent of selling six Premium Starter Kits with no additional work!

Earning your first share is your first business goal. Young Living's commission structure is based on the number of people and on volume. This creates a brilliant business model which positions you to succeed. You may already know your first three business partners or you may be looking forward to meeting them as you grow. Now, it's time to get your new business started right!

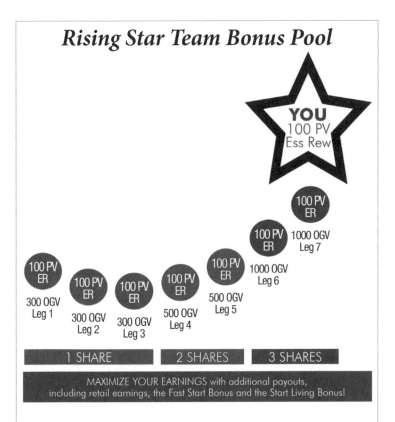

Rising Star Team Bonus Pool

YOU
100 PV
Ess Rew

100 PV ER

100 PV ER — 1000 OGV Leg 7

100 PV ER — 1000 OGV Leg 6

100 PV ER — 500 OGV Leg 5

100 PV ER — 500 OGV Leg 4

100 PV ER — 300 OGV Leg 3

100 PV ER — 300 OGV Leg 2

100 PV ER — 300 OGV Leg 1

1 SHARE   2 SHARES   3 SHARES

MAXIMIZE YOUR EARNINGS with additional payouts,
including retail earnings, the Fast Start Bonus and the Start Living Bonus!

Only Stars, Senior Stars, and Executives are eligible to earn shares based on 1% of all Young Living's monthly commissionable sales. The amount paid to the distributor is determined by the number of shares he or she earns. Qualifications:

1. Paid as a Star, Senior Star, or Executive
2. Have a 100 PV Essential Rewards order
3. Build three legs of at least 300 OGV each to qualify for one share. Add two legs of at least 500 OGV and receive two more shares. To earn three additional shares for an overall total of six, add two legs of at least 1,000 OGV each. Total possible shares is six.

Your First Business Goal

To build a strong, stable foundation under your business, you will need three business partners. Each of those partners must be in the Essential Rewards program and generate 300 OGV every month. This level of activity will earn you one share every month.

You'll succeed at this goal when you and three business partners each order 100 PV through the Essential Rewards (ER) program and each have an OGV of 300 PV.

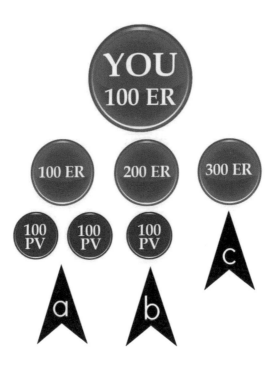

Here are just three of the ways you can maximize your shares each month.

a. One business builder makes a 100 PV ER order and enrolls two people who each purchase 100 PV. 100 PV+100 PV+100 PV= 300 OGV

b. One business builder makes a 200 PV ER order and whose customer makes a 100 PV order. 200 PV+100 PV= 300 OGV

c. One individual makes a 300 PV ER order. 300 PV= 300 OGV

How to Create a Six-Figure Income with Young Living

This explanation uses only Young Living "unilevel" earnings. This is the money you earn from your volume and does NOT include your Fast Start, Enroller or Rising Star Team Bonuses. This is also the correct structure for reaching the highest level in Young Living, Royal Crown Diamond.

Step 1: Building your first level

6 people @ 100 PV = 600 X 8% = $48/month

Step 2: Building your second level

36 people @100 PV= 3600 X 5% = $180

from level 2 + $48 from level 1 = $228/month

Step 3: Building your third level

216 people @ 100 PV = 21,600 X 4% = $864

from level 3 + $228 from levels 1-2 = $1092/mo.

Step 4: Building your fourth level

1,296 people @ 100 PV = 129,600 X 4% = $5,184

from level 4 +$1,092 from levels 1-3 = $6,276/month

Step 5: Building your fifth level

7,776 people @ 100 PV = 777,600 X 4% = $31,104

from level 5 +$6,276 from levels 1-4 = $37,380/month

This is $448,560 per year*

DISCLAIMER: There is no guarantee of earnings. No money is earned on the act of recruiting. All earnings are based on sales of product.

$100 of
Life-Giving
Products

I predict that Network Marketing will prove to be the most important solution to the current economic challenges facing the world today.

With the Young Living system as simple as each person purchasing $100 of their favorite life-giving products each month for the potential of enjoying a six to seven-figure annual earnings,

I simply cannot understand why everyone does not have a network. To me this is the most brilliant business model in the world today!

Teri Secrest

Now Let's Market! Ready, Set, Go!

As the CEO of your Young Living business, you are the OWNER of your own marketing company and Young Living is your client.

You are a marketing executive!

Marketing is the number one most important activity you will do in your business! My goal is to help you fall in LOVE with marketing!

Just as a building cannot stand on only one or two pillars, you cannot build a highly successful business with only one marketing activity. If you desire to build a highly successful business you must create a broad marketing strategy to keep your pipeline full of prospects.

Eight Pillars of Marketing

1. Classes & Referrals

Essential Oil Gatherings are the heart of our business. Why? Because when someone actually experiences an essential oil, it can have one of three effects on them rather quickly; The oils can have a physical effect, an emotional effect or a spiritual effect.

Essential oils really "sell" themselves! Our job is just to introduce them. Why not have a kickoff event to start your business?

Preparing for Your Kickoff Event!

Your kickoff event starts with a letter to your warm market. Your "warm market" is made of people who are friends, family and those you have a personal relationship with. These are the people who would listen to your recommendations because they know who you are. If you referred them to a great movie you saw or a restaurant where you've eaten, then consider them a part of your warm market.

Create a List of Your Warm Market Contacts

Create a list of everyone you can think of who is in your warm market. Use the Memory Jogger in the Appendix for ideas. Every time you meet someone who you feel would benefit from knowing about essential oils, be sure to add them to your list. Your list grows with your relationships and is constantly changing.

Creating Your Invitation List

Choose from your list the close friends and family members you want to invite to your kickoff event. Send them a Kickoff Invitation Letter.

Confirm Attendance

The day before your event, be sure to call each person who RSVP'd and confirm their attendance. Let them know how much you are looking forward to seeing them.

Sample Kickoff Invitation Letter

Dear [friend's name],

Hopefully, this finds you doing fabulous! This letter comes with some very exciting health news for you and your family. You may be aware that I have been using Young Living's life-giving products for some time now and I'm in the best health ever!

If you are looking for information to support your health, I would like to invite you to an exciting event at my home where you can sample my products and also hear about our exciting business partnerships.

Join me on [date] at [time]

We will be gathering at [address]

You must RSVP, as space is limited. Please call or email me to reserve your spot.

If, for some reason, you are not able to join me for this exciting experience, please e-mail or call me and I'd love to talk with you. Be sure to check out my website [your website URL] for great information on living a healthy lifestyle.

Warmly,

[your name]

[your website]

[your email address]

[your phone number]

P.S. As my business is rapidly expanding, if you know anyone looking for a fabulous home-based business, I would be so grateful to speak with them.

Preparing for Teaching Your Class

You will teach your entire class straight from the materials in your Premium Starter Kit, so you don't need to be an expert. In fact, it is better for your potential business builders if you aren't!

See Steps 1-6 below for the step-by-step class plan. Read through those steps several times while exploring your Premium Starter Kit, so you can easily find the materials and information you will share with your guests.

Look through the first section of your Product Guide to locate those pages that include the following information: company history, our farms, our Seed to Seal Process, What is an Essential Oil? and Three Ways to Use Essential Oils. You will be reading this information to your guests, so you may want to mark the pages.

In your kit you will also find a brochure that describes each of the essential oils in your Premium Essential Oil Collection. Read the information about each essential oil while opening, smelling and experiencing them. Take note of which oils are part of the Premium Essential Oil Collection and which is the bonus oil.

Taste the dietary oils, feel the topical oils and breathe in the aromatic oils. Take note of the essential oils you really love.

Practice Makes Perfect

Starting with Step 1 on page 79, hold up the Product Guide in front of the mirror and teach the class to yourself. Work your way through each subsequent step until you've practiced the entire class from beginning to end. Do this at least once before your first class. Saying the words out loud is very important.

Practice will help you to feel more comfortable and this will make your guests feel more welcome.

Call your upline and practice your class with him or her!

The following plan is wonderful for a class size of six to eight people. However, with just a few adjustments, you can share the same information at a one-on-one meeting as well as adjust it for a much larger audience.

Preparing Class Materials

Here is a list of the materials and samples I recommend you use for your class:

1. Essential Oil Premium Starter Kit
2. One Product Guide for each guest. Always staple your business card or place a printed label with your contact information on these Product Guides. They'll be shared an average of four times!

3. Business cards or printed labels with your contact information. Your guests need to bring your contact information home with them!
4. Printed order forms from your Virtual Office and/or a computer or tablet for taking orders.
5. Ningxia Red on ice and/or Slique® bars or other items that can be easily shared. (optional)
6. Thieves® soap, Young Living body lotion or any other products you'd like to share. (optional)

Setting Up the Room

The key to a successful class is helping each guest to have a positive essential oil experience. Start the experience right away by having your diffuser going. Use Thieves or Stress Away® in your diffuser. These two tend to be the most universally enjoyed.

Set out a glass water pitcher and glasses for your guests. Place bottles of Citrus Fresh™ and Lemon essential oil next to the pitcher and help your guests place a drop or two in their glass of water. You can talk about supporting healthy digestion and other body systems while they enter the room.

In your bathroom, have one of the Young Living hand soaps on your vanity for them to try. I've also placed a small tray of oils in my bathroom for guests to experience at their leisure.

When it comes to food, less is more. If you are going to serve a snack, serve something salty such

as nuts. Stay away from sweet snacks and desserts and food that is complicated to serve.

Teaching Your Class

Step 1: The Opening

Start your class by reading from your Product Guide the following sections. These facts are what sets Young Living apart from every other essential oil company.

- Our company and its history
- Our farms located all over the world
- Our seed to seal process
- What is an essential oil?
- Three ways to use essential oils

If you've visited the Young Living farm or attended a great company event, share your story about it at this time.

Step 2: Break out the Oils!

After your introduction, it's time to let your guests experience Young Living essential oils. Open your Premium Starter Kit and pull out each bottle. Refer to the essential oil information sheet located inside the kit and read right from it. Describe the oils as you pass them around the room.

Lead guests to flip through the entire Product Guide and notice all of the healthy lifestyle products Young Living offers. The product line goes beyond essential oils into oil-infused supplements, personal care products, green cleaning products and more. Give your guests an overview of these areas of Young Living and be sure to answer questions along the way.

Remember, we are not in the business of selling starter kits—we are introducing a healthy lifestyle to our guests which includes all aspects of Young Living.

While they're exploring the Product Guide, you may pass around the chilled Ningxia Red and the Slique bar samples, too. Open the Product Guide and find the pages on Ningxia Red and Slique. Read straight from those pages as well.

Step 3: Talking About the Premium Starter Kit

Show your guests the kit and let them know it includes all eleven oils in the Premium Essential Oil Collection and a free diffuser. Show them the sample bottles, cards and samples they will also receive. Explain that the kit includes a wholesale membership that will give them 24% off retail prices and—more than that—they get your support on their journey to health and wellness.

You also will benefit from making a "time-dated offer." This is something they get for buying their kit the night of the class. Think about your budget and your personality to decide what you may want to give away at your class for those who purchase a kit.

Understanding the Power
of Essential Rewards

Wholesale Member Discount

+

Essential Rewards Points

Month 1-6   Month 7-12   Month 13
                                        for Life

= Total Discount!

Step 4: Talking about Essential Rewards

Take a moment to talk about saving money and earning free products by enrolling in the Essential Rewards program. You actually are rewarded for making a commitment to your health! With every monthly autoship order, you save on shipping costs and earn points that you can redeem for free products! Plus, the longer you're enrolled in Essential Rewards, the great number of points you'll earn.

- From month one to month six, you receive 10% of your Essential Rewards order PV in points.
- From month seven to month twelve, you receive 15% of your Essential Rewards order PV in points.
- Beginning in month thirteen, you receive 20% of your Essential Rewards order PV in points for as long as you remain a member. With your wholesale member discount, your total discount is 44% discount. See the diagram entitled Understanding the Power of Essential Rewards.

Step 5: Growing Your Business

I recommend that you spend a few minutes talking about the business. Add something like this: "Finally, I want to be sure you are aware that Young

Living offers an awesome business opportunity.

If you would like to learn more about our business or would like to host a class, please let me know. If you know people who would benefit from what you learned tonight, I would be happy to teach a class for you. For more information about this, please come and see me right after the class."

Consider offering a special prize to the first person who books a class.

Step 6: The Close

At the end of the class let everyone know you are ready to take their order and help them get started. When you're collecting information from people, you should ask them, "Are you interested in the oils, the business or both?" This is another great way to see who may be interested in the business.

Referrals: Find a comfortable time during your class to ask for referrals. You will be delighted by how willing people are to give them to you. Go ahead and excuse those who need to leave and invite others to stay, ask questions and socialize a little.

Step 7: Review & Reflect

After your class is over, it is important to reflect on how it went. Ask yourself:
1. How many people were invited and how many

showed up?

2. How many guests purchased kits?
3. List three things you really liked about your event.
4. List three things you can improve.
5. Is there anything you'd like to add to the next class?
6. What do you need to print or order for your next event?
7. Do you feel like there is something you'd like to learn more about before your next event?

Reflection is an important part of growing and learning. Be sure to write down good notes on all of the ideas you have immediately following your class. You will be able to improve your event each and every time you do one.

2. Traveling Office

You want to be ready to do business any time, anywhere, so you'll find this traveling office very useful. Your traveling office can be as simple as the essential oil case on the right—just add your business cards, a pen and a small notepad—or as comprehensive as the large shoulder bag on the left. Fill your shoulder bag with the following:

1. Premium Starter Collection—just leave the diffuser in your car, in case you need it later

2. Clipboard with order forms

3. At least three Product Guides (your business card must be stapled to the front cover)

4. Postcards invitations for your next Introduction Class

5. Day planner for appointments

6. A few good business books to give out

Take your traveling office wherever you go. When you get into a great conversation with someone who would like more information about essential oils and other health products, you'll be well-equipped to give it to them. It will also be a constant reminder to keep your business at the forefront of your mind.

Your Cold Market is Heating Up!

These next six marketing activities are going to guide you into your cold market. These will, for the most part, be reaching people you don't know and have no relationship with.

A common mistake in cold market marketing is casting too wide of a net. You will have greater success when you focus your marketing on a single group of people called your niche market. The easiest market to reach is the one you connect with naturally. Generally, people tend to connect with those who range from ten years younger to ten years older than they are. The people in your niche market will often have the same marital status and be in the same season of life as you. You can certainly reach outside of that natural niche, but it would take research. I recommend starting with your natural niche market and pointing your marketing to it.

Ask yourself, "How would someone reach me?" and make a list of your answers.

Igniting the Entrepreneur in You

by Teri Secrest

Have you ever pondered what made America great in its early years? First and foremost, it was the unmerited favor of God. Now, we discover that men and women passionately embraced free enterprise. They started with a dream, rolled up their sleeves and didn't give up until their dream was achieved. American entrepreneurs developed more successful inventions and businesses in the last hundred years than in all the previous centuries put together.

Deep inside, each of us has a creative spark of genius that makes us completely unique. These creative ideas come straight from the heart of the Father. If we take the time to listen and act upon these ideas, we just may be on the verge of another entrepreneurial revolution.

Welcome to the heart of an entrepreneur. What about you? Have you ever had the burning desire to own your own business?

As a highly successful entrepreneur for over 35 years, I have had the privilege of mentoring hundreds of men and women in business. It gives me so much joy to see others excel. I would like to share five attributes that you can develop that are essential for maximum success in your business life.

Passion What makes you want to jump out of bed with enormous anticipation? If money were no object and you could do anything in the world, what would it be? What gives you more satisfaction and peace than anything else in the world? That is your passion. Don't ignore it. That is what you were born to do.

God put those desires in your heart. If you are fully surrendered to Christ, those passions are connected to your calling. Write them down, discuss them with a trusted friend and ask God for clarity.

Knowledge Decide to become more knowledgeable about your subject. Through reading and listening to experts in your area, you gain increasing confidence in your area of study.

You'll also develop decision-making ability about your dream and learn how to connect with people about your vision. Readers are leaders and leaders are readers. By investing just one hour a day in personal development, you gain seven hours a week in valuable skills and tools for developing your dream.

Courage Becoming fearless is the simple action of stepping out into new territory day after day after day. My secret to being fearless is that I have learned the value in laughing about my mistakes. Rather than allowing my mistakes to paralyze me, I use them to propel me forward. You can too!

Rapport All the knowledge in the world will not land you a million dollar business if you do not learn to connect with people in an authentic and sincere way. The first step to connecting with people is to become an impeccable listener. Listen with your whole heart every time someone speaks.

Persistence Persistence is closely tied to your passion. Once you have passion, then persistence can take you where you desire to go, even on the hard days. Identify the areas where you are facing obstacles. Perhaps it is a technical skill or a people skill. Then ask a trusted friend to be your accountability partner as you work through this obstacle. Every single obstacle has workable solutions. Purpose to get the word "can't" out of your vocabulary.

As you develop these five attributes, also remember the power of writing down your vision, your plan and the steps for reaching your goal.

My personal passion is helping people enjoy optimal health, so my business activities are focused in this area. When people try to get me off my life focus, I say "no."

So, what is your dream? If life has been hard and you have quit dreaming, think back to when you were very young and remember what you were naturally interested in and good at. It is never too late to start a business. In fact, this is probably the perfect season for you to begin. All you need is one good idea, tenacity and faith—always remember to keep your faith!

TERI SECREST has been a highly successful entrepreneur for 35 years. She owns four businesses: three traditional and one network marketing business. As one of the top 1% of women earners in America, Teri's heart is to see more believers embrace the biblical principles of business that made America great. Teri has authored numerous books and created DVDs and CDs on business and health. She has taught extensively on entrepreneurship in the US, Europe and Asia.

Choose topics that are also business-related in order to reach another audience.

3. Editorial Writing

Editorial writing is a great way to get exposure. Whatever area you have expertise in, begin writing articles that can help people. The article doesn't have to be about essential oils, but it should educate and add value to the life of readers everywhere.

Think about who you know that has a publication in your areas of expertise and interest. Head to the local health food store or bookstore and make a list of the magazines and publications that match your interest and niche market. Locally published magazines and newspapers are a starting place. Do an internet search and look for blogs and online publications as well. A blogger with a large number of readers can bring as much business as a national magazine.

Offer to be a guest writer by contacting the publications publisher or emailing the blogger. Many publications are always on the look out for new material to print.

Work 80% in your strength zone! If writing is not your passion, it's OK. There are many more pillars to choose from.

Editorial articles will help you reach people you may not reach otherwise. More than that, it's at no cost to you.

LET'S GET
WALKING
by *Teri Secrest*

CAN YOU THINK BACK to the last time you felt really good— I mean *really* good—as in full of energy, positive attitude and ready for the day? I'd like to share a simple secret with you that many well-respected people throughout history have discovered. It can literally elevate the way you feel physically and emotionally beginning today. It is *walking!*

Our beloved president, Abraham Lincoln, declared that he made some of his most important presidential decisions while walking the hills of Springfield.

Moses and Joshua were walkers, too. "So on that day Moses swore to me, 'The land on which your feet have walked will be your inheritance and that of your children forever, because you have followed the Lord my God wholeheartedly.'" (Joshua 14:9)

God created us to be walkers. Brisk walking is beneficial to every system in your body. It strengthens your cardiovascular system, cleans out your lungs, helps keep your hormones happy and, best of all, while you walk you take in oxygen which makes you feel better emotionally. Modern science has discovered that one of the greatest causes of depression is a lack of oxygen to the brain. By walking, you are proactively supporting your emotions on a daily basis.

As a personal health and wellness coach, one of the saddest things I see on a daily basis is the growing percentage of obesity in our youth population. This is tragic! We can change this. And it starts in our own homes with the choices we make. Even if you were raised in a family where your parents made unhealthy lifestyle choices, you can start a new legacy today. God's design for believers is that we walk in prosperity and health. "Beloved, I pray that you may prosper in all things and be in health, just as your soul prospers." (3 John 1:2)

As a result of daily walking, I feel better today than I did in my 20s, and so can you! God's design for us is not just longevity, but longevity with vitality.

Teri's Walking Tips

Invest in a good pair of walking shoes that give you support.

Talk to your family and friends. See if someone would like to be your *walking buddy*. (Don't let this stop you though. Your walking time can be your praying and creative-thinking time).

Start with a smaller commitment, such as 20 minutes 3 to 4 times per week. As you get stronger, work your way up to 45 minutes a day, 5 to 6 times per week.

Become very aware of *how* you are walking. By pushing off with your ankles as you step, you get more speed and a good rhythm.

Park far away from the store.

Take the stairs instead of the elevator.

Let me know how you're doing. I would love to hear from you as you get walking!

TERI SECREST is a certified wellness coach, health and business author and a highly successful entrepreneur. She has taught about health and kingdom business in the United States, Europe and Asia, and has appeared on over 50 radio and television shows.

4. Print Ads

Take the list of publications you created when looking at editorial articles. You may want to consider purchasing ad space in those publications. Before you consider a print ad, be sure the reach of the audience matches the financial investment. Make sure to choose one that reaches your niche market.

Print ads should always make the reader curious and want to know more. Here are just a few examples of some ads we have run. I highly encourage you to consider print marketing as an intermediate to advanced marketing push. It works well as a co-op where four to six people invest in the ad and share the leads. Full-page ads can be expensive and are best done with a shared expense.

The Power of a Small Ad

Do not underestimate the power of a small ad in a local newspaper. We once placed a business card-sized ad in a local faith-based newspaper. We actually ended up with only one response! That one contact ended up in a beautiful lifelong friendship. They are now a Young Living Platinum. Here is what the ad said: "Call today to discover the 6000 year-old ancient Biblical secrets of health".

Large photos are trending now.
An ad should create intrigue.

This ad creates both intrigue and curiosity.

5. Internet Business

The internet has expanded the face of networking and opened doors of business to people and markets once thought to be closed. Small towns, stay at home parents, and international business builders now have open doors to success. With consistent effort, anyone anywhere can create success.

The internet is a fabulous way to fill your lead pipeline. Just like the other forms of marketing, the fortune is in the follow up. As soon as you gain a new client convert that online relationship to a personal one as fast as possible. It's your personal relationships that will gain you clients for life.

Your Business Website

A website is the foundation of your internet business. This is where you will point your clients to on your internet ads. There are many duplicable websites already designed and available for Young Living business partners.

Starting With Social Media

TAKE IT SLOW! Only open accounts that you are comfortable with. If you are new to social media, start with one account, get success with it and then add another. If you already have accounts open, think about adding one at a time. Consistency with one social media account will yield a better return than inconsistent efforts over ten accounts. Some social media outlets to consider are Facebook, Twitter, Instagram, Gmail (for Google+ and YouTube), and Pinterest. Become familiar with the privacy practices of each company so you don't violate any rules.

Consistency is Key

Consistent posting is the most important aspect of your social media marketing. It is better to post once each day than it is to post seven times on one day.

When you post be highly relatable and create some really fun and relevant content. No one likes to read a post where they feel they're being sold. However, everyone likes really good information.

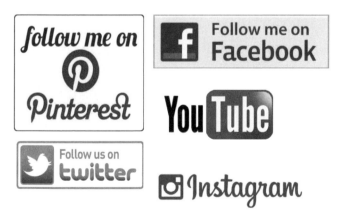

Elizabeth, Beverly and I often brainstorm
about our marketing.

Use the **70/20/10 Rule** when it comes to social
media posting. This ratio is good for any type of
social media.

- **70% of your posts should be information that
  is relevant to your niche market.** The Facebook
  audience Bev and I communicate with is mostly
  women who really like motivational quotes,
  videos and posts that inspire them to follow
  their dreams.
- **20% of your posts should be relevant specifi-
  cally to your product.** This could be the
  shareable graphics located in your Young living

virtual office. These posts should educate about essential oils, but not include a call to action.

- **10% of your posts should have a call to action**. These are your post you can use to ask "If you have been considering buying a Premium Starter Kit please give me a call or visit my website." Include a call to action. If you have been posting with the right ratio, your friends and family won't think twice about seeing a call-to-action post.
- Make sure to plan out your post topics to keep your ratio optimal.

You may use your planner or any of the social media planning tools out there such as HootSuite or Edgar. The upside to using a planning tool is that you can pre-schedule your posts. This means that you don't have to spend hours every single day trying to remember what you were going to post and when.

Some forms of social media, such as Facebook, have a planning tool already embedded in their system. However, a free tool like HootSuite allows you to plan for more than one form of social media at a time and will allow you to plan weeks ahead.

Facebook

I recommend starting with Facebook. People on Facebook tend to read a little bit more than those on other forms of social media. If you create a post that has good and interesting content, it will be readily shared by the Facebook community.

Keeping Information Private on Facebook

If you currently have a Facebook account, I recommend taking a look at the privacy settings. Some of you would rather keep personal moments and photos of family members separate from business postings, I recommend starting a private group called "Friends and Family." Pull into this group all of your contacts with whom you'd like to share your personal posts.

Also, when you make a personal post, you may change the distribution setting for that post to your Friends and Family. On the flip side, when you make a business post, you may exclude your Friends and Family group from seeing it. This should alleviate your concerns about casual acquaintances seeing private posts and overwhelming your family with business posts.

The best days and times to post on Facebook

How Often to Post

Begin posting once a day about something related to essential oils. But, because some Facebook audiences don't like an "over-poster," I suggest you limit your posts to once per day per Facebook group.

Where to Find Material for Your Posts

Don't be nervous about having to come up with your own content right away. Instead, look to your Young Living Virtual Office and become friends with your upline on Facebook. Also, you can use the Facebook search tool and search the words "Young Living." Begin following Young Living leaders on Facebook. This should give you essential oil posts that you can simply share.

As you read other posts and see what they say, start coming up with your own.

Setting up a Facebook Fan Page

Many business builders will set up a fan page for their business, which is very easy to do. It does have its limitations, however. You will be limited in your interactions with the "fans" who like your business page. Currently, you cannot personally interact with the people who like your fan page.

Setting up a Facebook Group

For these reasons and because network marketing is all about relationships, I have found that starting a Facebook group is much more effective and a great way to build your business. Here are the advantages:

- A group allows you to "friend" the people who become members.
- A Facebook group also allows the group members to talk to each other.
- You may post up questions and ask for answers.
- Members of the group are allowed to post also.

I have several Facebook groups that I run and post in. One group is just for my **business partners**, a place where we can easily communicate with each other. A Facebook group is also a great way to train your team.

In the beginning, you might not need a group like this, but as things get going and your organization starts to grow, it is wise to create a group for your team as a point of interaction.

Customer groups are a place where they can talk about essential oils and learn about the latest blends and essential oil-related news.

Topical groups are also a great way to build your clientele. Beverly started a group called "Being a Mom."

- In her group, 70% of her posts are mostly how-to tricks for moms with kids in school. She also posts a lot of recipes and cleaning tips.
- Her 20% consists of information about how essential oils help around the house and in life. For example, "A few drops of Purification inside those stinky athletic shoes can cut through any teenage smell."
- Her 10% changes depending upon her marketing goal.

"Sometimes, my goal is to get people to attend a live Internet class. In that case, I might say something like, 'If you have ever wanted to learn more about essential oils, please join me for my next Facebook virtual class,' and give them instructions on how to join.

Sometimes I will say, 'Visit my website' or 'If you have questions about essential oils, I'm happy to answer them. Please call me directly.'"

Virtual Classes

While live classes and one-on-one demonstrations are the best, virtual classes enable you to reach clients who live outside of your area and even all across the country.

There are several platforms you can use for virtual classes. Check out Facebook virtual classes via event pages and video, Google Hangout, Skype and Periscope.

Follow the same rules as in "How to Teach a Class" but you will describe each scent as opposed to passing around the bottle of oil. You'll find a great description of each scent on the information sheet in the Essential Oil Premium Starter Kit.

Blogging

Blogging is a great way to drive traffic to your website. There are a few duplicable website that come with blogs already included. If you select one that doesn't already include a blog, there are plenty of free options.

Blogger is the most simple option and it's free, but customization is limited. Wordpress starts free but can be less user-friendly. No matter what you choose, the goal of blogging is to create intriguing subject matter to draw readers to your website.

You'll want to write a new blog at least once per week. Post your blog on all of your social media accounts. You can post about your new blog more than once on Twitter. Create intriguing subject matter. Readers tend to be attracted to articles that include lists and numbers, for example, "3 Ways to Support Your Immune System."

YouTube

YouTube videos have changed the face of marketing forever! Think of YouTube as your video blog. YouTube videos are a great tool to reach new clients and to record information your new clients will like to see over and over. For example, making a YouTube video on the Starter Kit is a GREAT idea.

You can send your video to every new member and current clients.

Tips for Making Effective Videos

- First, keep your video short. You want to be under three to four minutes.
- Choose an appealing background.
- Check how you look before you shoot the video. There is nothing worse than a perfectly-executed video ruined by stray hair and bit of lunch between your teeth!
- Create compelling content with intriguing titles just like you would with a blog.
- Be sure to include your contact information and a strong call to action.

Twitter

Twitter is VERY fast-paced! You can post six times a day in Twitter and reach a different audience every time. The trick to Twitter is to have more than one account driving traffic to your website.

You will have to be very precise in your communication, as you are limited to 140 characters. It's almost like learning a new language.

The great thing about Twitter is you can really use it to promote your blog. You can post a URL right to it and readers can click through to read your blog. Pictures are also very useful tools because they stand out in the Twitter feed.

Think of Twitter as your promotion specialist. When you write your new blog, tweet about it. When you create a new video, tweet it out. Did you write a new newsletter? Tweet it. Did you wake up on the wrong side of the bed and have to start diffusing the essential oil of Joy just to think straight? Tweet it! The Twitter community is very casual and loves these types of communications.

Follow the 70/20/10 Rule on Twitter, too. Since you can post six times a day on Twitter, this means you can send a call to action every other day. In comparison, you'll only be sending calls to action about every ten days on Facebook. That's how different forms of social media work together to help your message get out to the world.

Pinterest

Pinterest is THE way to reach women! It's very visual. I recommend spending a little time on Pinterest to get a feel for what readers really like. There is a look and feel on Pinterest which is unique.

The best way to work Pinterest into your internet marketing is using it to promote your blog posts. Be sure to have an intriguing photo and "pin" it to one of your boards. As your followers see your pins, your blog will gain traction.

Pinterest users are very devoted and, if you catch their eye, they will return again and again. They will also re-pin your posts to their walls and introduce a brand new audience to your blog. Follow the same 70/20/10 Rule on Pinterest and be sure to like and re-pin other users' pins. This will get your face and username out there.

6. Market to Current Clients

I sincerely believe that every Young Living business owner can double their volume just by consistently marketing to their current clients. Some of the marketing activities that have helped us retain a long-term client base are:

- Monthly email newsletters
- Weekly short, automated emails
- Periodic contests with our clients
- Periodic postcards

Direct Mail

Give serious consideration to trying some direct marketing campaigns, because hardly anyone is doing direct mail marketing anymore.

Consider doing what other are not doing! Most people are only getting bills in the mail. How nice would it be to receive a thank you card?

Dear Young Living Friends,

Newsletters

Consider mailing newsletters to clients who don't have their email address on file. This is a great way to continue the education of your clients. Choose an intriguing subject or a promotion to build a newsletter around. It can even be your blog post! Print it and mail it out to your client. Send a newsletter once a month.

Postcards

Postcards cost the least to send through the mail. Young Living creates promotional postcards every month outlining that month's incentives. You can also create postcards about a single oil or other subject you find interesting. Once I sent a postcard to a prospect advertising an $11 product, and he called me with

You're Invited to experience a healthier lifestyle with Young Living Essential Oils

a $1600 order! He said that the postcard reminded him that he had one of my newsletters buried at the bottom of his desk! We use the postcard above to invite someone to our next introductory class.

Letters

Mail letters to remind clients of important changes. Young Living allows you to do a search for clients who are about to go inactive. Create a letter with an incentive for making that 50 PV order to stay active. Also consider mailing letters to clients that you have been unsuccessful in reaching via email.

7. Expos

Expos can be as simple as having a table at a Farmers Market each week or as elaborate as having a booth at a Women's Health Expo. Do your research, as some expos can be very expensive and more of an intermediate marketing landscape.

The key is to start conversations with as many people as possible, offer to let people experience our products and follow up with them quickly after the event. Avoid bringing a large supply of brochures, as they often just get thrown away by the attendees.

Expo Checklist

- Folding table and chairs
- Order forms on clipboards
- Information gather slips on clipboards
- Business cards
- Postcard invitations to next class/event
- Premium starter kit with diffuser
- Tablecloth
- Extension cord
- Tape: Duct tape, masking tape, scotch tape
- Scissors

If your expo is outside, think about having a pop-up overhead tent to shield you from the elements as well as having rocks to hold down any papers. Also consider your food and water needs.

At an expo, don't linger behind the table, but stand in front and engage in conversation with those who are walking by. Ask them, "Have you ever experienced essential oils?" Ask those who are interested if they would like to attend your local Essential Oil Intro class. The goal is to gather contact information and/or set up meetings.

8. Recognition

Recognition is one of the most important activities you can do to honor your team. Be very intentional about recognizing members who are committed to their business. Here is what I recommend:

Personally-Enrolled Members

Each time one of your personally-enrolled members makes a new rank, recognize them for it with a Facebook post. Place the recognition on their wall and any team wall you may have.

Stars and Senior Stars

Mail or email them a letter of congratulations about their new rank. Find out how they got there and show them how to get to the next level. You'd be surprised how many Stars and Senior Stars don't realize their business is growing. Recognize them on Facebook, too, which will help them market their business.

Executives

Think of something you can send them to help them grow their business. It can be gifting an app like Oily Tools, Simple Downline or Taxbot. Maybe make them some business cards.

Silver and Higher

By the time your business partner makes a leadership rank, you should know them really well. Ask them what they feel they need to make it to the next level and do what you can to provide it. We love sending roses to Silvers and above!

Activities for Builders on the Fast Track

Daily

Invest Thirty Minutes Into Self-Development

No one is born a leader or a good communicator; we all have areas to grow and learn in. Self-development is key to developing communication and leadership skills and growing into your Young Living business. Pick up some great self-development tools in those areas that excite you and set aside thirty minutes a day to spend on your education.

Never Stop Learning About Young Living

Watch a video on the compensation plan or watch someone conduct a class. Read the latest news or the Young Living blog. Do one thing every day to educate yourself on one aspect of Young Living, be it a product, the business or a new business tool.

Walk for Thirty Minutes

If you do other forms of daily exercise, consider this one done, but for those who have no regular regime, you need to get out and start walking first thing in the morning. Remember, this is good thinking time, planning time and even prayer time.

Check Your Business

Take a little time each day to login to your back office and see where you stand. Check your business legs and ask yourself if you need to make any calls to your leaders.

Weekly

Blogging

Creating fresh new blogs at least once a week is a wonderful way to get traffic to your essential oil website. Schedule time each week to write a new blog.

Teach an Essential Oils Introduction Classes

These classes can be offered once a week if you are on the fast track. From each oil class, you will invite them to the business opportunity class.

Teach a Business Opportunity Class

Business opportunity classes explain Young Living as a business to those interested in making their passion for our products into a business. Offering a business class once or week or twice a month can be very beneficial.

Ongoing Education Classes

You need to constantly be training your existing team, clients and customers. Ongoing education gives you that opportunity. Go beyond the oils and explore other areas of Young Living or choose a body system for each class. Keep that education coming. It's a good idea to teach these classes once or twice a month. So, if you're on the fast track, you will be teaching at least seven classes a month.

Check in With Your Upline

As your career develops and your team becomes larger and larger, you will be in constant contact with your top business builders. They will be checking in with you at least weekly to discuss their activities and challenges and to ask questions. If you live near each other, you may be teaching some classes together.

Business Builder Calendar: Fast Track

Monday	Tuesday	Wednesday	Thursday	Friday	Saturday	Sunday
	1 E-mail Newsletter	2 Send "Inactive" Letter	3 Ongoing Education Class	4 Social Media Scheduling	5 Send Recognition	6
7 Oils Introduction Class	8	9 Write New Blog Post	10 Business Opportunity Class	11 Social Media Scheduling	12	13
14 Oils Introduction Class	15	16 Write New Blog Post	17 Ongoing Education Class	18 Social Media Scheduling	19	20
21 Oils Introduction Class	22 >100-500 Calls	23 Write New Blog Post >100pv Calls	24 Business Opportunity Class	25 Social Media Scheduling Essential Reward Check	26 Mail newsletters to arrive by the 1st	27
28 Oils Introduction Class	29	30 Write New Blog Post				

Schedule Social Media

A social media presence is a wonderful way to reach into your cold market, introduce essential oils to your warm market and keep up with your current clients and team members. Pre-schedule all of your posts using a program like www.HootSuite.com so you don't have to be watching the clock and posting constantly.

Monthly

Email Newsletters

Every member of your organization should be receiving at least one email from you per month. That email is the newsletter. Choose some great new products to feature. Put in the promotions for the month. Always include your contact information and a section about Young Living as a business.

Inactive Notifications

Your back office gives you the ability to do a search for those who are about to have their accounts go inactive. Email those with an email address on file and mail those who do not. Let customers know that for a 50 PV order they can stay active.

Send Recognition

Wait until the fifth of the month to send recognition to your team for the previous month's work. This is when Young Living completes the final calculations and awards placements.

Printed Newsletters

These newsletters are simply printed versions of the newsletters you emailed out. Do a search using your virtual office to find those members without an email address on file. Mail a printable version of the newsletter to those who are not connected online to ensure that everyone receives continuing education regardless of internet connectivity. Include a small note in each asking your members to "go green" and put their email addresses on file.

Ensure Your Builders Receive Their Commissions

Your Virtual Office enables you to search for members of your organization who are at risk of missing their commissions for the month. Search for members with a PV of less than 100 (>100PV) and an OGV exceeding 500PV (<500).

When you see this combination, it is possible that your client could be leaving money on the table.

Your business builder may not know they missed the 100 PV mark or maybe they never planned to

have a business and one has started growing. You may be giving them some really good news and saving them from missing a check. Give these clients at least one call per month.

Essential Rewards

Do a check of those members you have on Essential Rewards to make sure their orders went through. If you see a day that has passed with no check mark by it, give them a call to make sure everything is going well.

Let Your Wave Begin

You now have a calendar of events to work from and eight marketing ideas to choose from—it's time to get started and grow. Let your business wave begin!

Identifying & Training Your Team

In this section, I will show you how to go from an accidental business to an intentional business and give you a step-by-step plan to educate your valued customers and train your new distributors. Early on, I recommend you begin to identify three business partners. You will know your business partners because they will:

1. Have a very strong "Why?"
2. Be enrolled in the Essential Rewards program.
3. Be committed to hosting classes and events.
4. Diligently follow up on any lead or client that you gift them.
5. Attend every company event in the area possible.

Once your first three business partners are trained and on their way to Young Living success, identify three more. You need a total of six business partners to maximize the Young Living compensation plan.

Training Your New Business Partners

Just like we talked about creating a marketing strategy, we also use a training platform for business builders. Please be sure to read my first book, *How to Be a Stunning Success in Network Marketing*, because I teach you how to play a "game of chess" with your new distributor.

Following are descriptions of all four phone trainings we use with new distributors.

Training #1

Hand your new business partner a copy of this book and open it to pages 48-49. Walk them through the first section, spending time with them on their "Why?" and writing it down.

Next, walk with them through making their time count and listing the life activities they find to be the most important. Help them choose their Young Living business hours.

Walk through the compensation plan all the way through the Rising Star Team Bonus, because that is their first business goal. How do they achieve that goal...through having a kickoff event! Just mention the event without too much detail. They can read through it on their own if they'd like.

You, as their mentor, need to give them their first two assignments: first, get a planner and second, fill out their Life & Business Plan. They need to fill out that plan and get it back to you before the second training session.

Training #2

Read their Life & Business Plan and analyze it. Does the number of hours they can work match their income goals? If not, be sure to discuss this with them. The two important points to discuss during this training are the first two marketing pillars. This is when you will discuss their kickoff event. Also, you'll need to talk about the five things every business builder does (see page 119). Find out if your new business partner is also doing these five activities and if not, discuss why.

Have your business partner put a professional voice message on their phone. This is a great way to get the word out about their new business. Help them set up their website. Once the website and phone message are complete, now you can construct the invitation to their kickoff event. Set the date for it. Set up your next training. The next one is all about practice.

Training #3

Have your new business partner practice the entire class from beginning to end. Talk to your new business builder about following up with each attendee the night before the event. Answer any questions they may have. The event is next! Training #4 occurs after the kickoff event.

If I live nearby, I often teach the first class, let my new business partner teach half of the next class and let them teach the entire third class while I observe. If their kickoff event is a virtual class, it works much the same way.

While classes are definitely the foundation of most business plans, there are exceptions. For example, if someone lives in a very rural area and cannot teach classes, you must help them create a business plan using the other marketing pillars to get their phones ringing.

Training #4

Time to reflect! Open this book to pages 84-85 and go over the questions with your business builder. What went well? What could be improved? The outcome of that event will determine which direction your training will go. Do they need help inviting people? Consider going over the Memory Jogger to help them come up with more people to invite. Did guests love the products and want classes taught at their homes? Let the event guide your mentorship.

Leveraging the Power of Your Team

The power of network marketing is leverage. Leveraging is pulling together the time and talents of everyone on the team to create lasting success for the whole team. You must train your team to be

strong and to train their team.

From Accidental to Intentional Business

If you are like many Young Living distributors, you fell in love with several of our products, began naturally telling friends about them—just like you would recommend a great restaurant—and suddenly you have an accidental business going!

That is what happened to me. In fact for many months, people kept trying to buy the products from me and I would turn them away and say, "No, I do not sell them, you need to call someone else!"

Young Living has the highest number of happy users I have ever seen in this industry. These customers usually purchase a wholesale membership because they love the discounted prices. They often share our products with a few people but generally, they are very faithful users. Take the best of care of this group. They rely on us for continuing education, new product updates and policy updates. Make sure you send them a newsletter at least once a month. Encourage them to put their email address on file with Young Living, as the company also does a good job of educating this group via email.

Strategies to Expand Your Communication Skills

Dr. Thomas W. Harrell, former professor at Stanford University, spent much of his career tracking a group of MBAs after graduation. He discovered that their grade point averages had little connection to their ultimate success in the business world—what really mattered were their social skills.

The graduates who ended up with the most prestigious jobs and the highest salaries were communicative, outgoing and energetic.

John Callen, a New York-based executive recruiter says, "The most sought-after skill, from CEO on down, is the ability to communicate with people." Prepare for success in marketing by expanding your communication skills.

1. Become an active and intentional listener

The following examples of listening are from the book, *Co-Active Coaching* by Henry Kimsey-House, Karen Kimsey-House, Philip Sandahl and Laura Whitworth.

Level 1 Listening

This is the lowest level of listening and it is entirely focused on ourselves. Even if we hear what the other person says, we are only paying attention to how what they say affects us.

Level 2 Listening— Focused Listening

Now you are tuning into their emotions, inflections, facial expressions and posture. This is called a level of empathy.

Level 3 Listening— Global Listening

This highest level of listening takes into account the action, inaction and interaction of the people involved but it also takes in the environment. So it relies heavily on the listener's intuition.

Performers, comedians, musicians, actors and

speakers have the ability to monitor how a room changes in response to what is said. If you desire to be a positive influence, you must enter into Level 3—Global Listening.

2. Learn to Ask Quality Questions

Good leaders ask questions that inspire others to dream more, think more, learn more, do more and become more. John Maxwell

Brian Tracy says,

> *"A major stimulant to creative thinking is focused questions."*

Our team has implemented the discipline of asking at least three questions of someone we are engaging in conversation before ever recommending our products or our business to them. Ask, listen, ask, listen, ask, listen and THEN respond.

3. Extend an Invitation

Using the example above, if someone comments about the beautiful scent you're wearing say something like "This is the essential oil of Joy. Do you have any experience with essential oils?"

Questions are a wonderful way to get conversations going. At the end, be sure to extend your invitation,

"I teach a class called An Introduction to Essential Oils. We are gathering at my home next Thursday; would you like to join us?" Take their contact information and be sure to invite them to your next class by handing them a postcard.

If the thought of speaking to people and inviting them to a class seems overwhelming, you may have an obstacle to overcome.

Obstacles stand between us and what we want for ourselves, our businesses and our families. If there is something keeping you for accomplishing what you'd like to do, there is hope!

Get Ready to Overcome Obstacles

What are the obstacles that are stopping you from success?

- A people skill
- A technical skill
- A family situation
- Your health
- Other big obstacles

Make a list of your biggest obstacles, reflect on what you can do to overcome each one and make a plan. Having an accountability partner is imperative to maximize your success.

Put your plan on your calendar and listen to classes, MP3s, audiobooks and online courses regularly. Never stop growing and developing.

Problem-Solving With Your Team

As leaders, we must always be looking forward for the sake of our team. Here are some questions you can ask when you know you have a problem, but do not know what the solution is.

- Why do we have this problem?
- How do we solve this problem?
- What specific steps must we take to solve this problem?

The more we ask for feedback from our team,

the more we can fine-tune our leadership skills and the more effective leaders we become. A question to always ask ourselves is, "Am I adding value to my team?" As we conclude this section on business, here are a few questions we can ask ourselves:

As a business owner, am I:

1. Adding value to my team?
2. Adding value to my customers?
3. Offering the best customer service possible?
4. Staying on the cutting edge of new technology?
5. Committed to growing as a person daily?
6. Keeping my priorities with family in line?
7. Passing on company updates to my team in a timely fashion?
8. Planning my time wisely?
9. Taking care of my physical health daily?
10. Becoming a better listener?

Section Three
How Big is Your Leadership Wave?

How Big Is Your Leadership Wave?

Within every person there is a natural-born desire to achieve something greater than themselves, something that will live on for future generations. Once you reach business success it is very natural to desire significance.

You were born to be a leader! Do you believe that? Some people have a quiet, gentle way of leading, yet they are still leaders! I believe you are drawn to this book because you are a born leader! It is just thrilling to be on this journey with you!

All noble dreams need a team. We cannot fully realize our dreams in life without a team! Network marketing is the best personal development program in the world because we have to learn how to be part of a team!

Ever since I was five years old, I knew that I was born to be an entrepreneur. Spearheading a marketing idea is so easy for me, I can do it in my sleep! What I did not know, however, is that entrepreneurs are not naturally-born leaders. Why? Because entrepreneurs often lack patience. We just want to get it done right now!

With all my enthusiasm for business, I thought people would just naturally love my ideas and want to follow. Absolutely not true! People do not respond just because you have a great idea, people respond because you are a great leader. No one cares how much you know, they only want to know how much you care.

By 2012, I was blessed to be in the top one percent of women earners in America. While I absolutely love and honor the abundance I enjoy, money is not my motivating factor. I love people! My heart's desire is to see many people reach a higher level of joy and fulfillment So I decided I needed to become a better leader!

Becoming a Good Leader
Always Starts on the Inside

As we become big on the inside, it begins to expand outward. It is much better to focus on growth than goals because inside growth produces goals.

I enrolled in an intensive, six-month leadership program offered by John Maxwell. After graduating from John's school, I then entered the next level of schooling, an intensive mentoring program. The difference this has made in both my personal life and my career life is astonishing.

Teri Secrest and John Maxwell at
Leadership Training

In 2015, <u>Inc.</u> magazine named John Maxwell the most influential leader in the world today and I believe they chose the right man. Several concepts I share in this chapter I have learned from John Maxwell.

Other great mentors whose ideas are represented here include Jim Rohn, Darren Hardy, Robert Kiyosaki, Dale Carnegie, Napoleon Hill and many more.

Who Are Your Heroes?

Think about some of the world changers that are living today and see who you identify with.

There is a pastor in Redding, California by the name of Bill Johnson, the Senior Pastor of Bethel Church.

Pastor Bill Johnson

When he was growing up, his father asked him the same question every night before he went to bed, "Son, is there something that God wants done that only you can do?" Today, Bill Johnson is one of the most influential faith leaders of our time.

The question I often text my children is this, "Did you do your best today?" They are probably thinking, "Mom, I've heard that a thousand times!" But I really believe, as the years go on, they will remember these word to live by.

In the following section we will explore some universal leadership principles which I believe can be a breakthrough moment for you.

Who Are Your Heroes?

Who are the people in your life that you look up to and identify with? Who would you like to be mentored by? What are the areas that you would like mentoring in? Write down your answers below.

_____

_____

_____

_____

_____

_____

_____

_____

_____

My Top Seven Cs of Leadership

1. Core Values

Our core values are our non-negotiable values that define who we are. By knowing who we are and what we value we will carry this understanding into each of our leadership decisions.

Take some time today and write down your top five core values. Share them with a loved one or trusted friend. Refer to them often.

Today's cultural trend would have us sway back and forth with the wind. While I wholeheartedly believe in accepting and loving all people, I respect my own core values and I am not afraid to let people know who I am. Let people know who you are. You will be surprised that most people will really respect you for it.

My Core Values Are

1.

2.

3.

4.

5.

2. Character

Character is the sum total of our everyday choices. It is consistency of values, ideals, thoughts, words and actions.

How can I see if my character needs a tune up?

John Maxwell suggests we ask ourselves these questions periodically:

1. Do you often miss deadlines?
2. Do you make resolutions and then go back to your old ways?
3. Do you place more importance on pleasing others than you do on maintaining the values you espouse?

4. Are you willing to shade the truth in order to get out of a tough spot?

5. Do you do what is easiest, even if you know it is not what's best?

6. Do other's show reluctance to trust you?

If you answered "Yes" to any of these questions, this is the perfect time to partner with a trusted friend and resolve these issues, so you can move towards maximum success!

3. Connecting

Until a few years ago, I thought communicating was the most important thing. In his book, *Everyone Communicates, Few Connect,* John Maxwell points out that, "Connecting authentically with someone includes both an intellectual and emotional connection."

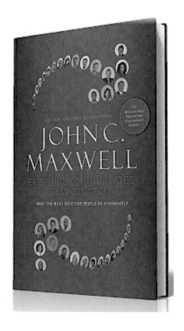

Here are some things I have personally learned that I hope will help you also.

- Let your team know how they have added value to your life.
- Be a trusted adviser to your clients
- The best question is, "Why?"
- Listen your way to common ground
- Be willing to share your failures with your team
- Seek to understand why your team member feels the way they do.

Connect! It will be well worth your time!

4. Courage

The higher you go in business the more courage you will need. I remember suggesting certain marketing campaigns where my team thought I was eccentric! Sometimes they were right! But ultimately, some of our most unusual marketing ideas, with high risk, have been very successful. Being courageous is looking at all the risks and then choosing to move forward on an idea. You must develop courage to go to the top in Young Living!

One of the most surprising things I have experienced about success is that there are people who just plain don't like you and don't care if you succeed. Being a people lover, this is so painful. It is nothing you can change. You just have to accept it and move on.

Courage is always taking the high road and always taking responsibility for your choices. People want to follow someone who is courageous!

5. Creativity

Creativity is paramount in good leadership! You must be able to think on your feet, be willing to change directions if it is for the good of the project, and you must be able to spearhead productive brainstorming sessions with your team.

People who are too rigid lose their creativity, and in my opinion, often disqualify a good idea in favor of an old idea.

Business does not work the same today as it did twenty years ago. Just because you have "always done it this way", does not make it the best way.

If you feel you lack creativity, consider taking an art class or doing something outside of the box for you. You are going to need all the creativity possible to lead your team to the top!

6. Confidence with Humility

Being confident in yourself and your ability is a very positive quality for a leader. People want to follow someone who is confident. Just be sure that you allow others to shine and that you acknowledge and honor the achievements of your team often!

Being confident with humility is acknowledging others who have helped you become who you are.

7. Clarity About Your Calling

One of the most challenging things you can face as your success grows is that people put many expectations on you. People are always asking you to do this or fly there or support this or that cause. I was not ready for this when it happened! At times, you do not feel like your life is your own anymore. That is when you discover that you must gain clarity on your calling and focus on your vision. If you are not clear on your path in life, someone else will choose your path for you!

Taking time each day for thinking and reflecting has helped me stay grounded in my calling and allowed me to be more effective in helping people.

You may have to say, "No, thank you," a lot more, but your "Yeses" to the right opportunities will make you a more effective leader.

A Final Note About the Seven Cs

If you focus on one of these Cs each day for seven days, I believe it will greatly benefit you. This is also a great exercise to do with your team for a week. Discuss one of these principles on your Facebook group each day for a week and just share thoughts and ideas. We can learn so much from each other!

Developing leadership skills is a lifelong endeavor, so jump in for the long haul! If you can find a buddy partner or an accountability partner to go on this journey with you, it is even better. The key is, don't let anything or anyone talk you out of your decision to grow!

There are very few true leaders in the world. Those who do not have a vision to lead will be your biggest critics and they will do everything imaginable to bust your enthusiasm. Write down your vision to lead and let nothing sway you otherwise!

Five Vital Qualities of an Effective Leader

1. Leaders are Readers

If you desire to be a good leader, develop a love for reading! Leaders are readers and readers are leaders. If your schedule does not allow large amounts of time for you to read, get your books on tape or on MP3s. I read everything with a yellow highlighter in hand marking everything that really stands out for me. Then I read through two more times all the highlighted notes until the information really becomes a part of my life and my actions. You just cannot go wrong with any of John Maxwell's seventy books on leadership.

I used to think that good leaders are good teachers. What I have discovered over thirty-five years of business is that good leaders ask good questions! The more questions you ask, the more information you receive and the more real communication that takes place.

When you have an opportunity to sit down with someone you admire or respect in business, always have a list of questions that you are ready to ask them and be prepared to take good notes.

My all-time favorite one is *15 Invaluable Laws of Growth*. This would be a great book for a study group with your team!

2. Leaders Are Willing to Correct Their Flaws

You may be wondering why it is so hard to lead ourselves? Because we all have blind spots that prevent us from seeing where we have problems and fall short. A blind spot can be an addiction, a weakness, our ego, innocence, failure to pay attention to details and much more.

This is why we all need accountability partners. This person loves you unconditionally and will tell you the truth, in love, about your blind spots. They offer support and solutions. Never try to do Network Marketing alone, because you cannot reach maximum success alone and it is no fun!

3. Leaders Choose their Attitude

The primary cause of the results we are getting in business is our attitude. We must be willing to shift our emphasis from the effect of our experiences to the cause of them!

Zig Ziglar says, "It's your attitude not your aptitude, that will determine your altitude". To become a truly good leader we must be willing to take 100% responsibility for every action in our lives.

I love this quote from Christian Simpson: "Life is a mirror which reflects back at you whatever you put into it. Life brings to you what you bring to life! If your business profits and the quality of your life are not where you intend them to be, it is time to check in with yourself." It is never to late to shift something that is not working.

4. Leaders Don't Make Excuses

Excuses shrink our stature. Be congruent and dependable. We are not always perfect but we must always be honest!

5. Leaders Lead Well At Home

As you develop as a leader, your capacity to affect your culture also expands! Affecting a culture starts right at home. There is an old saying that I whole heartedly agree with, "The hand that rocks the cradle rules the world."

Has anyone out there ever struggled with the mundane parts of parenting? The endless dishes, endless cleaning up, and sometimes thankless days? As much as I absolutely love and adore each of my children, there were times when I struggled with parenting. The logistics of where we lived made it impossible to travel and do a lot of the things I love.

Finally I decided to surrender! I purposed to make parenting the most fun thing I had ever done! This one shift in attitude changed everything! Women, we have an awesome opportunity to shape the culture of our homes. We get to be in charge of the beauty, the music, the atmosphere and whether or not we create a safe haven for other children. This is a treasure we have been given. It is never too late to mobilize this gift, but it is easier if we begin when our children are young. Whatever age your children are, start today!

We started a family tradition at Christmas time which has continued for the last fourteen years! People come over with large amounts of food and we sing around the piano for hours and hours! These traditions bring stability, anticipation and thoughtfulness to the neighborhood, and before you know it, you have started your own small cultural wave!

Fathers, in the ancient tradition it was very common for the father to speak a blessing over his children on a regular basis. The power of these words of blessing is so great that it cannot be measured.

Just as we desire to create a very large cultural wave, your blessing can begin a cultural wave in your children as well.

Mentoring the Next Generation

Every day, ask yourself two questions: "What am I learning?" and "Can I pass it on?" How ever many hours a week you work, consider mentoring someone else 10% of that time. So during your forty-hour week, mentor someone else for four hours a week.

Create your cultural wave by mentoring the next generation!

- Mentor people who are hungry.
- Mentor people who are accountable.
- Mentor people who report back to you what they learned and what they are doing with what they learned.

The minute you learn something, teach it to someone else. You will learn it better yourself, and it will bless the other person.

Stepping Into a Life of Significance

As we purpose to add value, to educate and to inspire people every day, our wave of influence will grow organically and we will not need to think about our legacy—our legacy will take care of itself.

Once you have reached significance in your life, success will no longer satisfy you, but you must first reach success.

If we see life through a filter of love, hope, anticipation and abundance, others around us will begin to view life this way and our cultural wave will grow.

Young Living is a great company to be aligned with because they are deeply committed to training up the next generation and they support many important causes around the world.

If someone tells you their dream, ask them what kind of a team they have around them. You have to have a dream and a team! If you have great people around you, they will take you higher than your dream!

My Three Greatest Secrets of Success

In closing, I would like to share the three greatest secrets of my success in business.

First, when I made the decision to create a successful Young Living business, I had no business background, no advertising dollars, no upline, and no computer for the first four years. I made a core decision to invite God to be my CEO and my active business partner. It was the best decision I ever made, just a simple invitation to the Creator of the universe to walk with me in this journey.

Often, I get amazing solutions to marketing questions in the middle of the night that I simply could not figure out on my own! Often during my morning walk, new ideas come flooding in that just amaze me! I believe our Heavenly Creator just loves being a daily part of our business! You can enjoy his help, too, just by asking.

Second, many years ago I learned the principles of tithing a minimum of 10% of my income back to the Lord's work. I decided to follow this principle and have also found that it is simply impossible to out-give the good Lord.

I think it is so sad when church people complain about giving 10% back to the Lord. I say He owns it all anyway and He continually lavishes good things on those who honor Him. The tithing principle is a universal principle regardless of what your particular religious persuasion is. It is a principle that sets into motion a blessing on those who give from their heart.

My third secret to success involves you! The absolute secret to your success is becoming the best one-of-a-kind you! So do not waste one minute trying to be like anyone else... invest every waking minute getting to know, love, and accept yourself. Then, work hard, be diligent, do your best, and let God do the rest!

It is such a privilege to share my thirty-five years of business success with you and I am believing for your maximum success in Young Living and in your life!

Are you ready to Brave Your Wave? Let's do it together!

To your success with Love,

Teri Secrest

Ten Ways to Exceed Expectations in Your Work and Your Life!
by John Maxwell

Only 2% of the world exceeds expectations in life and business. If you will be consistent and exceed expectations, you will own the field!

1. If you desire to create a big leadership wave, you need to LOVE where you are right now! Love what you do both before and after you are successful. Cultivate an attitude of gratitude in every stage of life and you will really enjoy the journey!

2. Show up early and leave late!

3. Expect more from yourself than you do from others.

4. Do not live off your past glories! Purpose to continue growing and learning today and purpose to add value to people every day! Yesterday ended last night!

5. Don't use relationships to cover up shortcomings or flaws. If you are doing a job for a friend, you should actually do more.

6. Ask for feedback all the time! We see ourselves through our intentions, but others see us as we really are. Ask someone,

7. "How did I do?" and "What am I missing?" The greatest compliment you can give someone is to ask their opinion.

8. Only travel the high road with others. The low road is selfish and your own interests come first. The middle road is, "I will treat you nice if you treat me nice." The high road is, "I'm going to treat you better than you treat me!"

9. Give 100% at key times during the day; be aware of your energy flow. Be your best when it really counts. Use your low energy times for less significant things. Bring people around you who also desire to exceed expectations.

10. Every day, do something for someone that is not expected of you!

Life & Business Plan

Please complete and send to your sponsor in advance of your business planning session.

Your contact information

Name	
Address	
City, State, Zip	
Daytime phone	
Evening phone	
Email	
Website	
Member #	

What is your current occupation?

What type of activities and tasks do you perform in your job?

Share your goals, dreams, and ideas about building a business:

What is your heart's desire for your life? What is your mission–that dream that's bigger than you, that lives on after you are gone? If money were no object, what would your life be like?

In order to fulfill your dreams:

How many hours per week are you willing to invest into your business? _____
When will those hours be? Between _____ and _____ o'clock

Are you willing to invest in your health and in your ability to demonstrate product benefits by purchasing product through the Autoship Program? Yes _____ No_____

Are you willing to invest operating capital each month?
If so, how much? Circle one: $50 $100 $150 $200 $250

Life & Business Plan
Page 2

Are you willing to invest in a Leads Generation program each
month to grow your business?
If so, how much? Circle one: $50 $100 $150 $200 $250
If so, what type(s)? Circle: TV   Radio   Ad Campaigns   Internet

What are your seven greatest strengths?

In what three areas do you feel you need assistance?

Do you have the capability of working on the internet?
Circle those that apply: Computer   Internet   Email
Facebook Twitter Pinterest Blogging Other

Do you have interest in building your business on the internet?
Strong interest_____ Some interest_____ No interest _____

What is your experience/comfort level in navigating the internet
and communicating via email?
Experienced_____ Some experience _____ Inexperienced _____

What monthly income would you like to be earning with your
business?
In six months $_____ In one year $_____ In three years $_____

In what three local markets would you be interested in working
to build your business?

Market 1 _____
Market 2 _____
Market 3 _____

Thank you!
Please forward your completed plan to me via email.
We'll call to schedule a time for your planning session.

Creating Your Warm Market List

My Personal Memory Jogger

Keeping track of all of your prospects in one place allows you to measure your progress in contacting them.

So who do you know? First fill in the names and then go back and look up their phone numbers.

Once you speak with someone, mark off those you contact and add new names to the bottom. You'll be surprised by just how many people you'll come up with to invite to your kickoff event and beyond.

I recommend starting with those closest to you first and inviting them to your kick-off event. Then start working through your Memory Jogger list in sets of fifteen. Send out fifteen letters, follow up with them and then send out fifteen more. That is a great way to keeping your pipeline full of prospects.

I suggest you grab a Ningxia Red, add a shot of Ningxia Nitro and just have fun with this process!

- Members of your own family
- Your closest friends
- Closest business associates
- Friends and neighbors
- Co-workers
- Church members
- Hobby buddies
- Fishing, hunting friends
- Workout friends

Those you do business with:
- Auto mechanic
- Accountant
- Banker
- Child care provider
- Car dealer
- Dentist and doctor
- Dry cleaner
- Grocer/Gas station attendant
- Hair stylist/barber
- Housekeeper
- Insurance agent
- Lawyer
- Merchants
- Pharmacist
- Real Estate Agent
- Travel Agent

Who are my ...?
- Architect
- Associations members
- Bus driver
- Butcher/Baker
- Computer tech
- Children's friends parents
- Chiropractor
- Club members
- Delivery person
- FedEx/UPS Driver

- Fireman
- Florist
- Fundraiser
- Furniture Salesman
- Gardener
- Golfer
- Government worker
- Graphic Artist
- Hairdresser
- Handyman
- Health Practitioner
- Hiker
- Hospital staff
- Human Resources staff
- Insurance Agent
- Internet provider
- Interior Decorator
- Jeweler
- Lab Technician
- Lawyer
- Leasing Agent/Manager
- Loan Officer
- Medical Professional
- Manager
- Massage Therapist
- Mechanic
- Minister
- Nurse
- Nutritionist
- Pet Care Professional
- Physical Therapist
- Police
- Property Manager
- Sports Team members
- Tailor
- Veterinarian
- Waitresses/Waiter

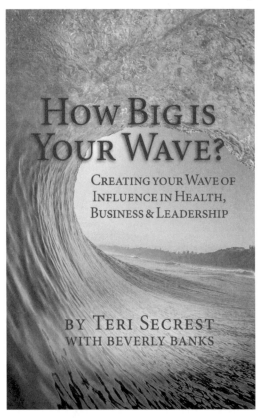

Books by Teri Secrest

Now available in English, German & Spanish!

The business model known as network marketing is the most misunderstood and under-rated business in the world today. While critics waste valuable time trying to discredit the industry, the industry continues to produce successful entrepreneurs worldwide while traditional businesses continue to lose profits, downsize employees and fire those close to retirement age.

My passion is educating people on how to make smart business decisions that will positively affect their bottom line for generations.

About the Author

Teri Secrest is a highly successful entrepreneur for the past thirty-five years and one of the top 1% of women earners in America today. Teri has been a guest on over fifty international radio and television shows and is a sought-after speaker on business and healthy lifestyles. Teri has lectured across the globe on business and health including the United States, Europe, and Asia.

Teri's heart is to be an ambassador to the nations, bringing people and ideas together to help individuals reach their highest potential! She believes that even the most challenging life history can become the most victorious life destiny!

Teri is a Royal Crown Diamond with Young Living Essential Oils. She resides with her family in Florida.